studysync®

Reading & Writing Companion

Divided We Fall

Why do we feel the need to belong?

studysync®

studysync.com

Send all inquiries to:
BookheadEd Learning, LLC
610 Daniel Young Drive
Sonoma, CA 95476

ISBN 978-1-94-469591-0

4 5 6 LMN 24 23 22 21 20

B

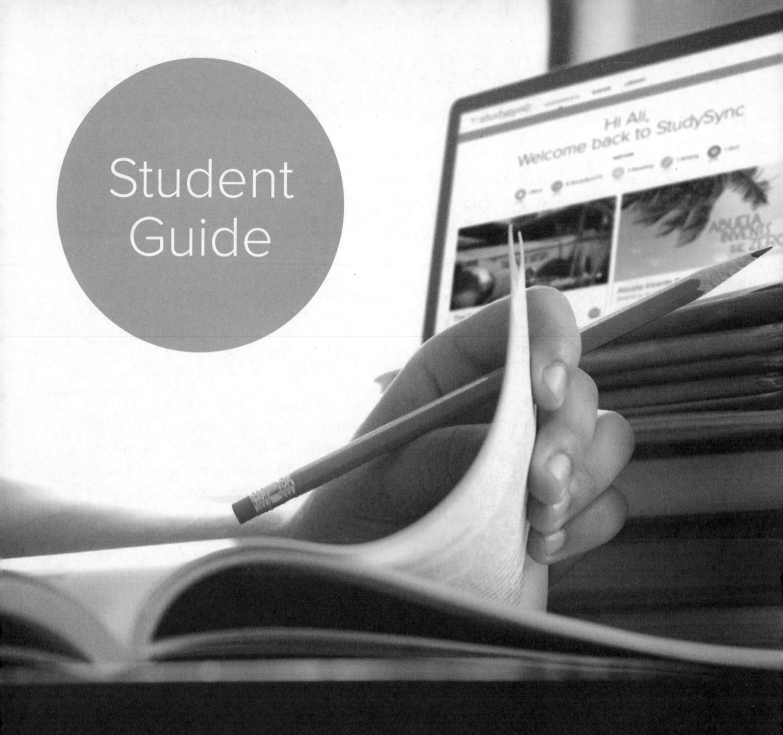

Student Guide

Getting Started

Welcome to the StudySync Reading & Writing Companion! In this book, you will find a collection of readings based on the theme of the unit you are studying. As you work through the readings, you will be asked to answer questions and perform a variety of tasks designed to help you closely analyze and understand each text selection. Read on for an explanation of each section of this book.

Close Reading and Writing Routine

In each unit, you will read texts that share a common theme, despite their different genres, time periods, and authors. Each reading encourages a closer look through questions and a short writing assignment.

Marigolds
FICTION
Eugenia Collier
1969

Introduction

studysync

ugenia Collier (b. 1928) is a writer and educator from Baltimore, Maryland, who is best known for this powerful short story, which received the Gwendolyn Brooks Prize for Fiction. Growing up in a Depression-era town, Lizabeth, the narrator of "Marigolds," recalls two things: the dusty air of her childhood, and a moment in her adolescence that changed her life forever. Confused and amused by why the town outcast, Miss Lottie, puts so much care into the brilliantly colored patch of marigolds outside her crumbling gray shack, Lizabeth and her friends tease the old woman and throw rocks at her flowers. A later incident in the garden causes Lizabeth great shame, but leads to a deeper moral understanding.

Marigolds

> "A little cloud of dust followed our thin legs and bare feet as we tramped over the barren land."

When I think of the hometown of my youth, all that I seem to remember is dust—the brown, crumbly dust of late summer—arid, sterile dust that gets into the eyes and makes them water, gets into the throat and between the toes of bare brown feet. I don't know why I should remember only the dust.

Great Depression-Era shantytown, 1936

Surely there must have been lush green lawns and paved streets under leafy shade trees somewhere in town; but memory is an **abstract** painting—it does not present things as they are, but rather as they *feel*. And so, when I think of that time and that place, I remember only the dry September of the dirt roads and grassless yards of the shantytown where I lived. And one other thing I remember, another incongruency of memory—a brilliant splash of sunny yellow against the dust—Miss Lottie's marigolds.

Whenever the memory of those marigolds flashes across my mind, a strange nostalgia comes with it and remains long after the picture has faded. I feel again the chaotic emotions of adolescence, illusive as smoke, yet as real as the potted geranium before me now. Joy and rage and wild animal gladness and shame become tangled together in the multicolored skein of fourteen-going-on-fifteen as I recall that devastating moment when I was suddenly more woman than child, years ago in Miss Lottie's yard. I think of those marigolds at the strangest times; I remember them vividly now as I desperately pass away the time.

Skill
Textual Evidence

I can quote these details as support for the claim that Lizabeth's destructive actions were motivated in part by the poverty around her. They show a history of poverty and suggest that there is little hope

1 Introduction

An Introduction to each text provides historical context for your reading as well as information about the author. You will also learn about the genre of the text and the year in which it was written.

2 Notes

Many times, while working through the activities after each text, you will be asked to **annotate** or **make annotations** about what you are reading. This means that you should highlight or underline words in the text and use the "Notes" column to make comments or jot down any questions you have. You may also want to note any unfamiliar vocabulary words here.

You will also see sample student annotations to go along with the Skill lesson for that text.

Reading & Writing Companion

③ First Read

During your first reading of each selection, you should just try to get a general idea of the content and message of the reading. Don't worry if there are parts you don't understand or words that are unfamiliar to you. You'll have an opportunity later to dive deeper into the text.

④ Think Questions

These questions will ask you to start thinking critically about the text, asking specific questions about its purpose, and making connections to your prior knowledge and reading experiences. To answer these questions, you should go back to the text and draw upon specific evidence to support your responses. You will also begin to explore some of the more challenging vocabulary words in the selection.

⑤ Skills

Each Skill includes two parts: Checklist and Your Turn. In the Checklist, you will learn the process for analyzing the text. The model student annotations in the text provide examples of how you might make your own notes following the instructions in the Checklist. In the Your Turn, you will use those same instructions to practice the skill.

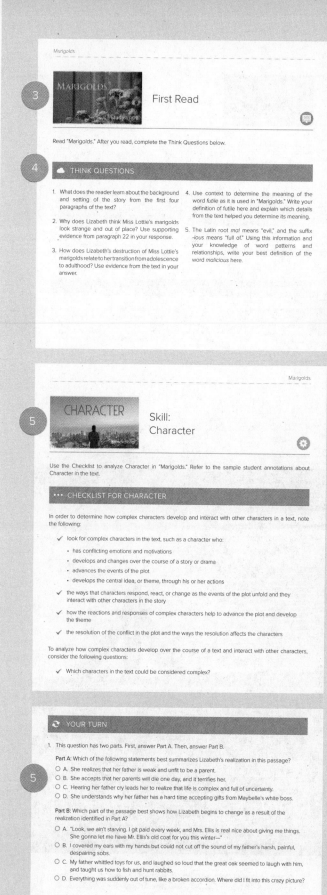

MARIGOLDS

Close Read

Study work

6

Reread "Marigolds." As you reread, complete the Skills Focus questions below. Then use your answers and annotations from the questions to help you complete the Write activity.

⊙ SKILLS FOCUS

1. Identify a passage in the beginning of "Marigolds" in which narration is used to reveal Lizabeth's character. Explain how it shows her complexity.

2. Identify a passage in the middle of the text in which the author uses imagery, or mental pictures created by descriptive and figurative language, to depict the setting. Explain how this language helps readers visualize the place being described in vivid terms.

3. Identify a passage in the dialogue between Lizabeth's parents that helps convey their characters. Describe how the passage helps show that the characters have believable personalities and emotions.

4. Find the passage near the end of the story when Lizabeth lashes out in Miss Lottie's yard. How does she interact with the setting of the story? Explain how Lizabeth's actions reveal her emotions.

✏ WRITE

7

NARRATIVE: Imagine that a grown-up Lizabeth is granted the opportunity to return and apologize to Miss Lottie, explaining why she destroyed the marigolds. Write a narrative that focuses on the dialogue that takes place between these two characters, years after the events described in the story. To prepare, review textual details and descriptions of Lizabeth's childhood world, how her feelings developed over the course of the text, her motivations and interactions, and consider how they influenced her devastating actions.

Please note that the excerpts and passages in the StudySync® library and this workbook are intended as instructions to generate interest in an author's work. The excerpts and passages do not substitute for the reading of entire texts, and StudySync® strongly recommends that students seek out and purchase the whole literary or informational work in order to experience it in the author intended. Links to online retailers are available in our digital library. In addition, complete works may be ordered through an authorized reseller by filling out and returning to StudySync® the order form enclosed in this workbook.

Reading & Writing Companion 🖥 **17**

8

The Christmas Truce of 1914

INFORMATIONAL TEXT

Introduction

World War I was a disastrous war, full of unimaginable agony among the troops. However, early in the war, a remarkable truce occurred. What was it that made enemy troops, for a short while, stop fighting and become friends?

8

▼ VOCABULARY

trench
long ditch used by soldiers to stay safe and hidden

truce
an agreement between enemies to stop fighting

tacitly
in a way that is understood or agreed without speaking a word

mutiny
refusal to accept orders; a rebellion

6

Close Read & Skills Focus

After you have completed the First Read, you will be asked to go back and read the text more closely and critically. Before you begin your Close Read, you should read through the Skills Focus to get an idea of the concepts you will want to focus on during your second reading. You should work through the Skills Focus by making annotations, highlighting important concepts, and writing notes or questions in the "Notes" column. Depending on instructions from your teacher, you may need to respond online or use a separate piece of paper to start expanding on your thoughts and ideas.

7

Write

Your study of each selection will end with a writing assignment. For this assignment, you should use your notes, annotations, personal ideas, and answers to both the Think and Skills Focus questions. Be sure to read the prompt carefully and address each part of it in your writing.

8

English Language Learner

The English Language Learner texts focus on improving language proficiency. You will practice learning strategies and skills in individual and group activities to become better readers, writers, and speakers.

Extended Writing Project and Grammar

This is your opportunity to use genre characteristics and craft to compose meaningful, longer written works exploring the theme of each unit. You will draw information from your readings, research, and own life experiences to complete the assignment.

1 Writing Project

After you have read all of the unit text selections, you will move on to a writing project. Each project will guide you through the process of writing your essay. Student models will provide guidance and help you organize your thoughts. One unit ends with an **Extended Oral Project** which will give you an opportunity to develop your oral language and communication skills.

2 Writing Process Steps

There are four steps in the writing process: Plan, Draft, Revise, and Edit and Publish. During each step, you will form and shape your writing project, and each lesson's peer review will give you the chance to receive feedback from your peers and teacher.

3 Writing Skills

Each Skill lesson focuses on a specific strategy or technique that you will use during your writing project. Each lesson presents a process for applying the skill to your own work and gives you the opportunity to practice it to improve your writing.

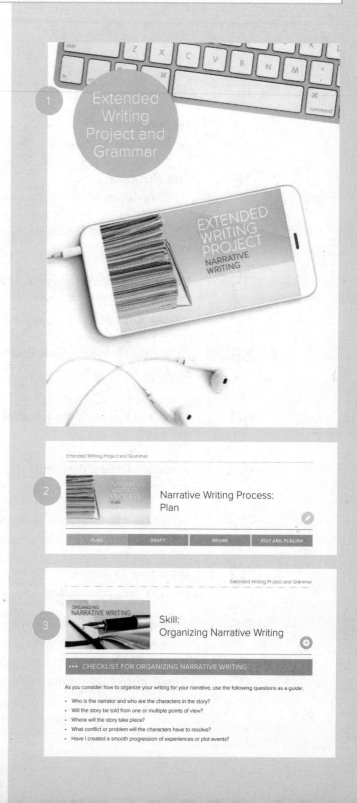

Divided We Fall

Why do we feel the need to belong?

Genre Focus: FICTION

Texts

 Paired Readings

1   **Marigolds**
FICTION *Eugenia Collier*

18   **The Necklace**
FICTION *Guy de Maupassant*

32   **Metamorphoses (Jupiter, Lycaon)**
POETRY *Ovid*

35   **Braving the Wilderness: The Quest for True Belonging and the Courage to Stand Alone**
INFORMATIONAL TEXT *Brené Brown*

39   **St. Lucy's Home for Girls Raised by Wolves**
FICTION *Karen Russell*

60   **Sure You Can Ask Me a Personal Question**
POETRY *Diane Burns*

63   **Angela's Ashes: A Memoir**
INFORMATIONAL TEXT *Frank McCourt*

72   **Why I Lied to Everyone in High School About Knowing Karate**
INFORMATIONAL TEXT *Jabeen Akhtar*

83   **Welcome to America**
POETRY *Sara Abou Rashed*

86   **I Have a Dream**
ARGUMENTATIVE TEXT *Martin Luther King Jr.*

97   **The Future in My Arms**
INFORMATIONAL TEXT *Edwidge Danticat*

Extended Writing Project and Grammar

102 | Plan

Organizing Narrative Writing

109 | Draft

Story Beginnings
Narrative Techniques
Narrative Sequencing
Descriptive Details
Conclusions

123 | Revise

Grammar: Prepositions and Prepositional Phrases
Grammar: Independent and Dependent Clauses
Grammar: Basic Spelling Rules I

132 | Edit and Publish

English Language Learner Resources

134 | The Christmas Truce of 1914
         | INFORMATIONAL TEXT

143 | When Everything Changed
         | POETRY

155 | Text Fulfillment through StudySync

Unit 1: Divided We Fall

Why do we feel the need to belong?

JABEEN AKHTAR

Jabeen Akhtar is a Pakistani American author who was born in London and immigrated to the United States with her family when she was two years old. Akhtar has spent much of her life in Washington, DC, where she worked for the federal government for ten years before writing her first novel, *Welcome to Americastan* (2011). She frequently publishes essays on topics ranging from animal rights activism to politics to the portrayal of South Asian characters in American comics.

BRENÉ BROWN

Social scientist Brené Brown (b. 1965) is an author and research professor at the University of Houston. Through her work, including a top-viewed TED talk entitled "The Power of Vulnerability," Brown sparks conversation about courage, belonging, and empathy. Brown was the oldest of four children born in San Antonio, and her family lived in both New Orleans and Houston as she grew up. She often writes about her own experiences, and writes in her book *The Gifts of Imperfection,* "Owning our story can be hard but not nearly as difficult as spending our lives running from it."

EUGENIA COLLIER

Eugenia Collier (b. 1928) is an American writer, critic, and dramatist who worked as a caseworker at the Baltimore Department of Public Welfare prior to her forty-year career as a professor of English. When Collier was growing up during the Great Depression in Baltimore, she lived with her parents and a rotating cast of tenants in her grandparents' three-story house. Her work employs a range of voices and often addresses family relationships and failed social systems.

EDWIDGE DANTICAT

Known for her realistic portrayal of Haitian culture, Edwidge Danticat (b. 1969) bases much of her work on her own life and history. Danticat's novels and short stories tackle themes related to place and identity. In works like *The Farming of Bones* (1999), her novel recounting the 1937 massacre of Haitian workers in the Dominican Republic, she considers how historical events continue to affect immigrants of the diaspora. In addition to writing, Danticat has worked with filmmakers Patricia Benoit and Jonathan Demme on documentaries about Haiti.

MARTIN LUTHER KING JR.

Dr. Martin Luther King Jr. (1929–1968), a Baptist minister and leader of the American civil rights movement, delivered his iconic "I Have a Dream" speech in 1963 from the steps of the Lincoln Memorial. It called for justice and equality for African Americans, who King declared still were not free a hundred years after the Emancipation Proclamation. King's speech strongly affected national opinion, resulting in the passage of the Civil Rights Act of 1964, which ended segregation in public places and employment discrimination.

GUY DE MAUPASSANT

Guy de Maupassant (1850–1893) was a French author who was known as a master of the short story; many of which take place during the Franco-Prussian war in the 1870s and express an antiwar sentiment. His story "The Necklace" was imitated by the writer Henry James in his story "Paste" and by Somerset Maugham in "Mr. Know-it-All" and "A String of Beads." He published over three hundred short stories during his lifetime, as well as several novels, three travel books, and one volume of poetry.

FRANK MCCOURT

Frank McCourt's (1930–2009) bestselling memoir *Angela's Ashes* (1996) documents the Irish American author's childhood of extreme poverty growing up in the slums of Limerick, Ireland, in the 1930s. The book, McCourt's first, won the Pulitzer Prize in 1997 and was translated into seventeen languages. His next two memoirs focused on his experiences as an Irish immigrant and public school teacher in New York City.

SARA ABOU RASHED

Sara Abou Rashed (b. 1999) moved with her family to Columbus, Ohio, in 2013 to escape the war in Syria. Her poetry, which she often performs as spoken word, addresses themes related to immigration and identity. In 2015, just two years after starting to learn English, she won the Ohio Poetry Association High School Contest and the Columbus City Poetry Slam.

KAREN RUSSELL

Karen Russell (b. 1981) has published three short story collections and a novel, and her work is often discussed alongside writers of magical realism and speculative fiction. Born and raised in Miami, Russell cites her close relationship with her siblings as a template for the themes and preoccupations her characters (who are usually kids and teenagers) explore. The author grew up reading science fiction and fantasy novels and loved visiting theme parks like the Miami Seaquarium and Parrot Jungle.

DIANE BURNS

Born in Lawrence, Kansas, to a Chemehuevi father and an Anishinabe mother, poet Diane Burns (1956–2006) grew up in Riverside, California. In the 1980s she established herself as a fixture in New York City's Lower East Side poetry community, performing in legendary establishments such as the Bowery Poetry Club and the Nuyorican Poets Café. Her only poetry collection, *Riding the One-Eyed Ford* (1981), explores Native American identity and stereotypes.

OVID

Ovid (43 BCE–17 CE) was one of the best-known poets in the Roman Empire, who abandoned a political career to write verse. A popular poet in his time, Ovid's signature was to reinvent himself, and the genre, with each work. His 12,000-line poem, the Metamorphoses (8 CE), put new form to old stories and has been refigured and fashioned in literature of every period of history since. Ovid was exiled that same year by the Emperor Augustus to the island of Tomis on the Black Sea.

Marigolds

FICTION
Eugenia Collier
1969

Introduction

Eugenia Collier (b. 1928) is a writer and educator from Baltimore, Maryland, who is best known for this powerful short story, which received the Gwendolyn Brooks Prize for Fiction. Growing up in a Depression-era town, Lizabeth, the narrator of "Marigolds," recalls two things: the dusty air of her childhood, and a moment in her adolescence that changed her life forever. Confused and amused by why the town outcast, Miss Lottie, puts so much care into the brilliantly colored patch of marigolds outside her crumbling gray shack, Lizabeth and her friends tease the old woman and throw rocks at her flowers. A later incident in the garden causes Lizabeth great shame, but leads to a deeper moral understanding

"A little cloud of dust followed our thin legs and bare feet as we tramped over the barren land."

Copyright © BookheadEd Learning, LLC

1   When I think of the hometown of my youth, all that I seem to remember is dust—the brown, crumbly dust of late summer—arid, sterile dust that gets into the eyes and makes them water, gets into the throat and between the toes of bare brown feet. I don't know why I should remember only the dust. Surely there must have been lush

Great Depression-Era shantytown, 1936

green lawns and paved streets under leafy shade trees somewhere in town; but memory is an **abstract** painting—it does not present things as they are, but rather as they *feel*. And so, when I think of that time and that place, I remember only the dry September of the dirt roads and grassless yards of the shantytown where I lived. And one other thing I remember, another incongruency of memory—a brilliant splash of sunny yellow against the dust— Miss Lottie's marigolds.

2   Whenever the memory of those marigolds flashes across my mind, a strange nostalgia comes with it and remains long after the picture has faded. I feel again the chaotic emotions of adolescence, illusive as smoke, yet as real as the potted geranium before me now. Joy and rage and wild animal gladness and shame become tangled together in the multicolored skein of fourteen-going-on-fifteen as I recall that devastating moment when I was suddenly more woman than child, years ago in Miss Lottie's yard. I think of those marigolds at the strangest times; I remember them vividly now as I desperately pass away the time.

3   I suppose that **futile** waiting was the sorrowful background music of our impoverished little community when I was young. The Depression[1] that gripped the nation was no new thing to us, for the black workers of rural Maryland had always been depressed. I don't know what it was that we were

---

1. **The Depression** the period in the 1930s when America and other countries experienced a devastating economic downturn

Skill: Textual Evidence

I can quote these details as support for the claim that Lizabeth's destructive actions were motivated in part by the poverty around her. They show a history of poverty and suggest that there is little hope of change.

NOTES

NOTES

waiting for; certainly not for the prosperity that was "just around the corner," for those were white folks' words, which we never believed. Nor did we wait for hard work and thrift to pay off in shining success, as the American Dream promised, for we knew better than that, too. Perhaps we waited for a miracle, **amorphous** in concept but necessary if one were to have the grit to rise before dawn each day and labor in the white man's vineyard until after dark, or to wander about in the September dust offering one's sweat in return for some meager share of bread. But God was chary with miracles in those days, and so we waited—and waited.

4   We children, of course, were only vaguely aware of the extent of our poverty. Having no radios, few newspapers, and no magazines, we were somewhat unaware of the world outside our community. Nowadays we would be called culturally deprived and people would write books and hold conferences about us. In those days everybody we knew was just as hungry and ill clad as we were. Poverty was the cage in which we all were trapped, and our hatred of it was still the vague, undirected restlessness of the zoo-bred flamingo who knows that nature created him to fly free.

5   As I think of those days I feel most poignantly the tag end of summer, the bright, dry times when we began to have a sense of shortening days and the imminence of the cold.

6   By the time I was fourteen, my brother Joey and I were the only children left at our house, the older ones having left home for early marriage or the **lure** of the city, and the two babies having been sent to relatives who might care for them better than we. Joey was three years younger than I, and a boy, and therefore vastly inferior. Each morning our mother and father trudged wearily down the dirt road and around the bend, she to her domestic job, he to his daily unsuccessful quest for work. After our few chores around the tumbledown shanty, Joey and I were free to run wild in the sun with other children similarly situated.

7   For the most part, those days are ill-defined in my memory, running together and combining like a fresh watercolor painting left out in the rain. I remember squatting in the road drawing a picture in the dust, a picture which Joey gleefully erased with one sweep of his dirty foot. I remember fishing for minnows in a muddy creek and watching sadly as they eluded my cupped hands, while Joey laughed uproariously. And I remember, that year, a strange restlessness of body and of spirit, a feeling that something old and familiar was ending, and something unknown and therefore terrifying was beginning.

8   One day returns to me with special clarity for some reason, perhaps because it was the beginning of the experience that in some inexplicable way marked the end of innocence. I was loafing under the great oak tree in our yard, deep

Skill:
Character

Lizabeth shares how her hatred of poverty was vague and undirected. This suggests that she has pent up anger that might impact her future choices. I'm going to pay close attention to her behavior to see if any of it is driven by her anger.

in some reverie which I have now forgotten, except that it involved some secret, secret thoughts of one of the Harris boys across the yard. Joey and a bunch of kids were bored now with the old tire suspended from an oak limb, which had kept them entertained for a while.

9   "Hey, Lizabeth," Joey yelled. He never talked when he could yell. "Hey, Lizabeth, let's go somewhere."

10   I came reluctantly from my private world. "Where you want to go? What you want to do?"

11   The truth was that we were becoming tired of the formlessness of our summer days. The idleness whose prospect had seemed so beautiful during the busy days of spring now had degenerated to an almost desperate effort to fill up the empty midday hours.

12   "Let's go see can we find some locusts on the hill," someone suggested.

13   Joey was scornful. "Ain't no more locusts there. Y'all got 'em all while they was still green."

14   The argument that followed was brief and not really worth the effort. Hunting locust trees wasn't fun anymore by now.

15   "Tell you what," said Joey finally, his eyes sparkling. "Let's us go over to Miss Lottie's."

16   The idea caught on at once, for annoying Miss Lottie was always fun. I was still child enough to scamper along with the group over rickety fences and through bushes that tore our already raggedy clothes, back to where Miss Lottie lived. I think now that we must have made a tragicomic spectacle, five or six kids of different ages, each of us clad in only one garment—the girls in faded dresses that were too long or too short, the boys in patchy pants, their sweaty brown chests gleaming in the hot sun. A little cloud of dust followed our thin legs and bare feet as we tramped over the barren land.

17   When Miss Lottie's house came into view we stopped, ostensibly to plan our strategy, but actually to reinforce our courage. Miss Lottie's house was the most ramshackle of all our ramshackle homes. The sun and rain had long since faded its rickety frame siding from white to a sullen gray. The boards themselves seemed to remain upright not from being nailed together but rather from leaning together, like a house that a child might have constructed from cards. A brisk wind might have blown it down, and the fact that it was still standing implied a kind of enchantment that was stronger than the elements. There it stood and as far as I know is standing yet—a gray, rotting thing with

Please note that excerpts and passages in the StudySync® library and this workbook are intended as touchstones to generate interest in an author's work. The excerpts and passages do not substitute for the reading of entire texts, and StudySync® strongly recommends that students seek out and purchase the whole literary or informational work in order to experience it as the author intended. Links to online resellers are available in our digital library. In addition, complete works may be ordered through an authorized reseller by filling out and returning to StudySync® the order form enclosed in this workbook.

Reading & Writing Companion   3

NOTES

no porch, no shutters, no steps, set on a cramped lot with no grass, not even any weeds—a monument to decay.

18   In front of the house in a squeaky rocking chair sat Miss Lottie's son, John Burke, completing the impression of decay. John Burke was what was known as queer-headed. Black and ageless, he sat rocking day in and day out in a mindless stupor, lulled by the monotonous squeak-squawk of the chair. A battered hat atop his shaggy head shaded him from the sun. Usually John Burke was totally unaware of everything outside his quiet dream world. But if you disturbed him, if you intruded upon his fantasies, he would become enraged, strike out at you, and curse at you in some strange enchanted language which only he could understand. We children made a game of thinking of ways to disturb John Burke and then to elude his violent retribution.

19   But our real fun and our real fear lay in Miss Lottie herself. Miss Lottie seemed to be at least a hundred years old. Her big frame still held traces of the tall, powerful woman she must have been in youth, although it was now bent and drawn. Her smooth skin was a dark reddish brown, and her face had Indian-like features and the stern stoicism that one associates with Indian faces. Miss Lottie didn't like intruders either, especially children. She never left her yard, and nobody ever visited her. We never knew how she managed those necessities which depend on human interaction—how she ate, for example, or even whether she ate. When we were tiny children, we thought Miss Lottie was a witch and we made up tales that we half believed ourselves about her exploits. We were far too sophisticated now, of course, to believe the witch nonsense. But old fears have a way of clinging like cobwebs, and so when we sighted the tumbledown shack, we had to stop to reinforce our nerves.

20   "Look, there she is," I whispered, forgetting that Miss Lottie could not possibly have heard me from that distance. "She's fooling with them crazy flowers."

21   "Yeh, look at 'er."

22   Miss Lottie's marigolds were perhaps the strangest part of the picture. Certainly they did not fit in with the crumbling decay of the rest of her yard. Beyond the dusty brown yard, in front of the sorry gray house, rose suddenly and shockingly a dazzling strip of bright blossoms, clumped together in enormous mounds, warm and passionate and sun-golden. The old black witch-woman worked on them all summer, every summer, down on her creaky knees, weeding and cultivating and arranging, while the house crumbled and John Burke rocked. For some perverse reason, we children hated those marigolds. They interfered with the perfect ugliness of the place; they were too beautiful; they said too much that we could not understand; they did not make sense. There was something in the **vigor** with which the old woman destroyed the weeds that intimidated us. It should have been a comical

NOTES

sight—the old woman with the man's hat on her cropped white head, leaning over the bright mounds, her big backside in the air—but it wasn't comical, it was something we could not name. We had to annoy her by whizzing a pebble into her flowers or by yelling a dirty word, then dancing away from her rage, reveling in our youth and mocking her age. Actually, I think it was the flowers we wanted to destroy, but nobody had the nerve to try it, not even Joey, who was usually fool enough to try anything.

23 "Y'all git some stones," commanded Joey now and was met with instant giggling obedience as everyone except me began to gather pebbles from the dusty ground. "Come on, Lizabeth."

24 I just stood there peering through the bushes, torn between wanting to join the fun and feeling that it was all a bit silly.

25 "You scared, Lizabeth?"

26 I cursed and spat on the ground—my favorite gesture of phony bravado. "Y'all children get the stones, I'll show you how to use 'em."

27 I said before that we children were not consciously aware of how thick were the bars of our cage. I wonder now, though, whether we were not more aware of it than I thought. Perhaps we had some dim notion of what we were, and how little chance we had of being anything else. Otherwise, why would we have been so preoccupied with destruction? Anyway, the pebbles were collected quickly, and everybody looked at me to begin the fun.

28 "Come on, y'all."

29 We crept to the edge of the bushes that bordered the narrow road in front of Miss Lottie's place. She was working placidly, kneeling over the flowers, her dark hand plunged into the golden mound. Suddenly *zing*—an expertly aimed stone cut the head off one of the blossoms.

30 "Who out there?" Miss Lottie's backside came down and her head came up as her sharp eyes searched the bushes. "You better git!"

31 We had crouched down out of sight in the bushes, where we stifled the giggles that insisted on coming. Miss Lottie gazed warily across the road for a moment, then cautiously returned to her weeding. *Zing*—Joey sent a pebble into the blooms, and another marigold was beheaded.

32 Miss Lottie was enraged now. She began struggling to her feet, leaning on a rickety cane and shouting. "Y'all git! Go on home!" Then the rest of the kids let loose with their pebbles, storming the flowers and laughing wildly and

Skill:
Character

I see that Lizabeth's pent up anger causes her to attack Miss Lottie in this section because it makes her feel powerful. Her actions here drive the actions of other characters, so Lizabeth will definitely have an effect on the plot of the story.

Skill:
Text-Dependent Responses

Lizabeth feels ashamed of what she did with her power and is unable to laugh with the younger children. Her inner child, who says to laugh it off, and her inner adult, who feels guilt, are in conflict.

senselessly at Miss Lottie's impotent rage. She shook her stick at us and started shakily toward the road crying, "Git 'long! John Burke! John Burke, come help!"

33 Then I lost my head entirely, mad with the power of inciting such rage, and ran out of the bushes in the storm of pebbles, straight toward Miss Lottie, chanting madly, "Old witch, fell in a ditch, picked up a penny and thought she was rich!" The children screamed with delight, dropped their pebbles, and joined the crazy dance, swarming around Miss Lottie like bees and chanting, "Old lady witch!" while she screamed curses at us. The madness lasted only a moment, for John Burke, startled at last, lurched out of his chair, and we dashed for the bushes just as Miss Lottie's cane went whizzing at my head.

34 I did not join the merriment when the kids gathered again under the oak in our bare yard. Suddenly I was ashamed, and I did not like being ashamed. The child in me sulked and said it was all in fun, but the woman in me flinched at the thought of the **malicious** attack that I had led. The mood lasted all afternoon. When we ate the beans and rice that was supper that night, I did not notice my father's silence, for he was always silent these days, nor did I notice my mother's absence, for she always worked until well into evening. Joey and I had a particularly bitter argument after supper; his exuberance got on my nerves. Finally I stretched out upon the pallet in the room we shared and fell into a fitful doze. When I awoke, somewhere in the middle of the night, my mother had returned, and I vaguely listened to the conversation that was audible through the thin walls that separated our rooms. At first I heard no words, only voices. My mother's voice was like a cool, dark room in summer—peaceful, soothing, quiet. I loved to listen to it; it made things seem all right somehow. But my father's voice cut through hers, shattering the peace.

35 "Twenty-two years, Maybelle, twenty-two years," he was saying, "and I got nothing for you, nothing, nothing."

36 "It's all right, honey, you'll get something. Everybody out of work now, you know that."

37 "It ain't right. Ain't no man ought to eat his woman's food year in and year out, and see his children running wild. Ain't nothing right about that."

38 "Honey, you took good care of us when you had it. Ain't nobody got nothing nowadays."

39 "I ain't talking about nobody else, I'm talking about *me*. God knows I try." My mother said something I could not hear, and my father cried out louder, "What must a man do, tell me that?"

NOTES

40   "Look, we ain't starving. I git paid every week, and Mrs. Ellis is real nice about giving me things. She gonna let me have Mr. Ellis's old coat for you this winter—"

41   "Damn Mr. Ellis's coat! And damn his money! You think I want white folks' leavings?"

42   "Damn, Maybelle"—and suddenly he sobbed, loudly and painfully, and cried helplessly and hopelessly in the dark night. I had never heard a man cry before. I did not know men ever cried. I covered my ears with my hands but could not cut off the sound of my father's harsh, painful, despairing sobs. My father was a strong man who could whisk a child upon his shoulders and go singing through the house. My father whittled toys for us, and laughed so loud that the great oak seemed to laugh with him, and taught us how to fish and hunt rabbits. How could it be that my father was crying? But the sobs went on, unstifled, finally quieting until I could hear my mother's voice, deep and rich, humming softly as she used to hum to a frightened child.

43   The world had lost its boundary lines. My mother, who was small and soft, was now the strength of the family; my father, who was the rock on which the family had been built, was sobbing like the tiniest child. Everything was suddenly out of tune, like a broken accordion. Where did I fit into this crazy picture? I do not now remember my thoughts, only a feeling of great bewilderment and fear.

44   Long after the sobbing and humming had stopped, I lay on the pallet, still as stone with my hands over my ears, wishing that I too could cry and be comforted. The night was silent now except for the sound of the crickets and of Joey's soft breathing. But the room was too crowded with fear to allow me to sleep, and finally, feeling the terrible aloneness of 4 A.M., I decided to awaken Joey.

45   "Ouch! What's the matter with you? What you want?" he demanded disagreeably when I had pinched and slapped him awake.

46   "Come on, wake up."

47   "What for? Go 'way."

48   I was lost for a reasonable reply. I could not say, "I'm scared and I don't want to be alone," so I merely said, "I'm going out. If you want to come, come on."

49   The promise of adventure awoke him. "Going out now? Where to, Lizabeth? What you going to do?"

50   I was pulling my dress over my head. Until now I had not thought of going out. "Just come on," I replied tersely.

51   I was out the window and halfway down the road before Joey caught up with me.

52   "Wait, Lizabeth, where you going?"

53   I was running as if the Furies[2] were after me, as perhaps they were—running silently and furiously until I came to where I had half known I was headed: to Miss Lottie's yard.

54   The half-dawn light was more eerie than complete darkness, and in it the old house was like the ruin that my world had become—foul and crumbling, a grotesque caricature. It looked haunted, but I was not afraid, because I was haunted too.

55   "Lizabeth, you lost your mind?" panted Joey.

56   I had indeed lost my mind, for all the smoldering emotions of that summer swelled in me and burst—the great need for my mother who was never there, the hopelessness of our poverty and degradation, the bewilderment of being neither child nor woman and yet both at once, the fear unleashed by my father's tears. And these feelings combined in one great impulse toward destruction.

57   "Lizabeth!"

58   I leaped furiously into the mounds of marigolds and pulled madly, trampling and pulling and destroying the perfect yellow blooms. The fresh smell of early morning and of dew-soaked marigolds spurred me on as I went tearing and mangling and sobbing while Joey tugged my dress or my waist crying, "Lizabeth, stop, please stop!"

59   And then I was sitting in the ruined little garden among the uprooted and ruined flowers, crying and crying, and it was too late to undo what I had done. Joey was sitting beside me, silent and frightened, not knowing what to say. Then, "Lizabeth, look!"

60   I opened my swollen eyes and saw in front of me a pair of large, calloused feet; my gaze lifted to the swollen legs, the age-distorted body clad in a tight cotton nightdress, and then the shadowed Indian face surrounded by stubby

---

Skill:
Textual Evidence

Details here support my claim that poverty led to Lizabeth's actions. They also support the idea that being an adolescent led to them. I know the confusion that comes with this age. I'll expand my claim to include both reasons.

2. **Furies** three female deities or spirits from Greek mythology that take vengeance or inflict punishment on mortals

Copyright © BookheadEd Learning, LLC

NOTES

white hair. And there was no rage in the face now, now that the garden was destroyed and there was nothing any longer to be protected.

61   "M-miss Lottie!" I scrambled to my feet and just stood there and stared at her, and that was the moment when childhood faded and womanhood began. That violent, crazy act was the last act of childhood. For as I gazed at the immobile face with the sad, weary eyes, I gazed upon a kind of reality which is hidden to childhood. The witch was no longer a witch but only a broken old woman who had dared to create beauty in the midst of ugliness and sterility. She had been born in squalor and lived in it all her life. Now at the end of that life she had nothing except a falling down hut, a wrecked body, and John Burke, the mindless son of her passion. Whatever verve there was left in her, whatever was of love and beauty and joy that had not been squeezed out by life, had been there in the marigolds she had so tenderly cared for.

62   Of course I could not express the things that I knew about Miss Lottie as I stood there awkward and ashamed. The years have put words to the things I knew in that moment, and as I look back upon it, I know that that moment marked the end of innocence. Innocence involves an unseeing acceptance of things at face value, an ignorance of the area below the surface. In that humiliating moment I looked beyond myself and into the depths of another person. This was the beginning of compassion, and one cannot have both compassion and innocence.

63   The years have taken me worlds away from that time and that place, from the dust and squalor of our lives, and from the bright thing that I destroyed in a blind, childish striking out at God knows what. Miss Lottie died long ago and many years have passed since I last saw her hut, completely barren at last, for despite my wild contrition she never planted marigolds again. Yet, there are times when the image of those passionate yellow mounds returns with a painful poignancy. For one does not have to be ignorant and poor to find that his life is as barren as the dusty yards of our town. And I too have planted marigolds.

 Skill: Text-Dependent Responses

As an adult, Lizabeth understands the full significance of the moment when Miss Lottie confronted her. It was the end of a childish innocence of seeing things at face value and the beginning of compassion.

Please note that excerpts and passages in the StudySync® library and this workbook are intended as touchstones to generate interest in an author's work. The excerpts and passages do not substitute for the reading of entire texts, and StudySync® strongly recommends that students seek out and purchase the whole literary or informational work in order to experience it as the author intended. Links to online resellers are available in our digital library. In addition, complete works may be ordered through an authorized reseller by filling out and returning to StudySync® the order form enclosed in this workbook.

Reading & Writing Companion   9

Skill:
Text-Dependent Responses

Use the Checklist to analyze Text-Dependent Responses in "Marigolds." Refer to the sample student annotations about Text-Dependent Responses in the text.

••• CHECKLIST FOR TEXT-DEPENDENT RESPONSES

In order to use textual evidence to support an appropriate response, ask the following:

- ✓ What is the question asking?

- ✓ What parts of the text are related to the question?

- ✓ What evidence from the text might support my response?

- ✓ What language from the question can I paraphrase in my response?

In order to write a text-dependent response, complete the following:

- ✓ **Read the question:**

  - Think about what you already know about the text that will help you answer the question.

  - Reread the question aloud, one sentence at a time if you're confused.

- ✓ **Reread and identify:**

  - Reread parts of the text that are relevant to the question.

  - Identify passages, quotations, and details in the text that will support your response.

  - Refer to your annotations for examples.

- ✓ **Write and Review:**

  - Use the language from the question to support your response.

  - Cite one or two pieces of evidence from the text to support your response.

  - Review your response to ensure you have answered the question in its entirety.

  - Proofread your response, checking for any spelling or grammatical errors.

 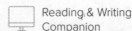

Skill:
Text-Dependent Responses

Reread paragraph 19 of "Marigolds." Then, using the Checklist on the previous page, answer the multiple-choice questions below.

🔄 YOUR TURN

1. Which piece of textual evidence supports the idea that the children are afraid of Miss Lottie?

   ○ A. "Miss Lottie seemed to be at least a hundred years old."
   ○ B. "She never left her yard, and nobody ever visited her."
   ○ C. "We never knew how she managed those necessities which depend on human interaction—how she ate, for example, or even whether she ate."
   ○ D. "But old fears have a way of clinging like cobwebs, and so when we sighted the tumbledown shack, we had to stop to reinforce our nerves."

2. Which piece of original commentary explains why the children are afraid of Miss Lottie?

   ○ A. Miss Lottie's isolated existence and intimidating presence make the children fear her.
   ○ B. Miss Lottie is a witch.
   ○ C. Miss Lottie is known for punishing children.
   ○ D. Miss Lottie cares more about her garden that she does about her son.

Please note that excerpts and passages in the StudySync® library and this workbook are intended as touchstones to generate interest in an author's work. The excerpts and passages do not substitute for the reading of entire texts, and StudySync® strongly recommends that students seek out and purchase the whole literary or informational work in order to experience it as the author intended. Links to online resellers are available in our digital library. In addition, complete works may be ordered through an authorized reseller by filling out and returning to StudySync® the order form enclosed in this workbook.

Reading & Writing
Companion

11

First Read

Read "Marigolds." After you read, complete the Think Questions below.

☁ THINK QUESTIONS

1. What does the reader learn about the background and setting of the story from the first four paragraphs of the text?

2. Why does Lizabeth think Miss Lottie's marigolds look strange and out of place? Use supporting evidence from paragraph 22 in your response.

3. How does Lizabeth's destruction of Miss Lottie's marigolds relate to her transition from adolescence to adulthood? Use evidence from the text in your answer.

4. Use context to determine the meaning of the word *futile* as it is used in "Marigolds." Write your definition of futile here and explain which details from the text helped you determine its meaning.

5. The Latin root *mal* means "evil," and the suffix *-ious* means "full of." Using this information and your knowledge of word patterns and relationships, write your best definition of the word *malicious* here.

Skill:
Textual Evidence

Use the Checklist to analyze Textual Evidence in "Marigolds." Refer to the sample student annotations about Textual Evidence in the text.

••• CHECKLIST FOR TEXTUAL EVIDENCE

In order to identify textual evidence to support your response, note the following:

✓ read the text closely and critically

✓ identify what the text says explicitly

✓ find the most relevant textual evidence that supports your analysis

✓ consider why an author explicitly states specific details and information

✓ cite the specific words, phrases, sentences, or paragraphs from the text that support your analysis

In order to interpret implicit meanings in a text by making inferences, do the following:

✓ combine information directly stated in the text with your own knowledge, experiences, and observations

✓ cite the specific words, phrases, sentences, or paragraphs from the text that led to and support this inference.

In order to cite textual evidence to support an analysis of what the text says explicitly as well as inferences drawn from the text, consider the following questions:

✓ Have I read the text closely and critically?

✓ What inferences am I making about the text?

✓ What textual evidence am I using to support these inferences?

✓ Am I quoting the evidence from the text correctly?

✓ Does my textual evidence logically relate to my analysis or the inference I am making?

Copyright © BookheadEd Learning, LLC

Skill:
Textual Evidence

Reread paragraphs 42 and 43 of "Marigolds." Then, using the Checklist on the previous page, answer the multiple-choice questions below.

⟳ YOUR TURN

1. Which textual evidence would best support a reader's claim that the conversation between Lizabeth's parents disrupts her perception of their respective roles in the family?

   - ○ A. I had never heard a man cry before.
   - ○ B. My father was a strong man who could whisk a child upon his shoulders and go singing through the house.
   - ○ C. But the sobs went on, unstifled, finally quieting until I could hear my mother's voice, deep and rich, humming softly as she used to hum to a frightened child.
   - ○ D. My mother, who was small and soft, was now the strength of the family; my father, who was the rock on which the family had been built, was sobbing like the tiniest child.

2. Which textual evidence would best support a reader's claim that the conversation between Lizabeth's parents disrupts her sense of belonging?

   - ○ A. I did not know men ever cried.
   - ○ B. I covered my ears with my hands but could not cut off the sound of my father's harsh, painful, despairing sobs.
   - ○ C. Everything was suddenly out of tune, like a broken accordion. Where did I fit into this crazy picture?
   - ○ D. I do not now remember my thoughts, only a feeling of great bewilderment and fear.

Skill:
Character

Use the Checklist to analyze Character in "Marigolds." Refer to the sample student annotations about Character in the text.

••• CHECKLIST FOR CHARACTER

In order to determine how complex characters develop and interact with other characters in a text, note the following:

- ✓ look for complex characters in the text, such as a character who:

  - has conflicting emotions and motivations

  - develops and changes over the course of a story or drama

  - advances the events of the plot

  - develops the central idea, or theme, through his or her actions

- ✓ the ways that characters respond, react, or change as the events of the plot unfold and they interact with other characters in the story

- ✓ how the reactions and responses of complex characters help to advance the plot and develop the theme

- ✓ the resolution of the conflict in the plot and the ways the resolution affects the characters

To analyze how complex characters develop over the course of a text and interact with other characters, consider the following questions:

- ✓ Which characters in the text could be considered complex?

- ✓ How do the characters change as the plot unfolds? When do they begin to change? Which events cause them to change? How do these changes advance the plot and develop the theme?

- ✓ How do the complex characters interact with other characters?

- ✓ How does the resolution affect the characters?

Please note that excerpts and passages in the StudySync® library and this workbook are intended as touchstones to generate interest in an author's work. The excerpts and passages do not substitute for the reading of entire texts, and StudySync® strongly recommends that students seek out and purchase the whole literary or informational work in order to experience it as the author intended. Links to online resellers are available in our digital library. In addition, complete works may be ordered through an authorized reseller by filling out and returning to StudySync® the order form enclosed in this workbook.

Reading & Writing
Companion

15

Skill:
Character

Reread paragraphs 35–43 of "Marigolds." Then, using the Checklist on the previous page, answer the multiple-choice questions below.

⟳ YOUR TURN

1. This question has two parts. First, answer Part A. Then, answer Part B.

   Part A: Which of the following statements best summarizes Lizabeth's realization in this passage?

   ○ A. She realizes that her father is weak and unfit to be a parent.

   ○ B. She accepts that her parents will die one day, and it terrifies her.

   ○ C. Hearing her father cry leads her to realize that life is complex and full of uncertainty.

   ○ D. She understands why her father has a hard time accepting gifts from Maybelle's white boss.

   Part B: Which part of the passage best shows how Lizabeth begins to change as a result of the realization identified in Part A?

   ○ A. "Look, we ain't starving. I git paid every week, and Mrs. Ellis is real nice about giving me things. She gonna let me have Mr. Ellis's old coat for you this winter—"

   ○ B. I covered my ears with my hands but could not cut off the sound of my father's harsh, painful, despairing sobs.

   ○ C. My father whittled toys for us, and laughed so loud that the great oak seemed to laugh with him, and taught us how to fish and hunt rabbits.

   ○ D. Everything was suddenly out of tune, like a broken accordion. Where did I fit into this crazy picture?

Close Read

Reread "Marigolds." As you reread, complete the Skills Focus questions below. Then use your answers and annotations from the questions to help you complete the Write activity.

◎ SKILLS FOCUS

1. Identify a passage in the beginning of "Marigolds" in which narration is used to reveal Lizabeth's character. Explain how it shows her complexity.

2. Identify a passage in the middle of the text in which the author uses imagery, or mental pictures created by descriptive and figurative language, to depict the setting. Explain how this language helps readers visualize the place being described in vivid terms.

3. Identify a passage in the dialogue between Lizabeth's parents that helps convey their characters. Describe how the passage helps show that the characters have believable personalities and emotions.

4. Find the passage near the end of the story when Lizabeth lashes out in Miss Lottie's yard. How does she interact with the setting of the story? Explain how Lizabeth's actions reveal her emotions.

✏ WRITE

NARRATIVE: Imagine that a grown-up Lizabeth is granted the opportunity to return and apologize to Miss Lottie, explaining why she destroyed the marigolds. Write a narrative that focuses on the dialogue that takes place between these two characters, years after the events described in the story. To prepare, review textual details and descriptions of Lizabeth's childhood world, how her feelings developed over the course of the text, her motivations and interactions, and consider how they influenced her devastating actions.

Please note that excerpts and passages in the StudySync® library and this workbook are intended as touchstones to generate interest in an author's work. The excerpts and passages do not substitute for the reading of entire texts, and StudySync® strongly recommends that students seek out and purchase the whole literary or informational work in order to experience it as the author intended. Links to online resellers are available in our digital library. In addition, complete works may be ordered through an authorized reseller by filling out and returning to StudySync® the order form enclosed in this workbook.

Reading & Writing Companion   17

The Necklace

FICTION
Guy de Maupassant
1884

Introduction

French author Guy de Maupassant (1850–1893) grew up wealthy but spent time among the working classes for much of his life. His classic short stories frequently depict ordinary people caught in disastrous or demeaning situations. Maupassant believed that writing should aim not at "telling a story or entertaining us or touching our hearts, but at forcing us to think about and understand the deeper, hidden meaning of events." "The Necklace" is one such story that asks readers to consider the true value of the things desired in life. Maupassant tells the story of a young Madame Loisel, a woman who is trapped in her daydreams until one fateful night.

"No; there's nothing more humiliating than to look poor among other women who are rich."

1   The girl was one of those pretty and charming young creatures who sometimes are born, as if by a slip of fate, into a family of clerks. She had no dowry[1], no expectations, no way of being known, understood, loved, married by any rich and distinguished man; so she let herself be married to a little clerk of the Ministry of Public Instruction.

2   She dressed plainly because she could not dress well, but she was unhappy as if she had really fallen from a higher station; since with women there is neither caste nor rank, for beauty, grace and charm take the place of family and birth. Natural ingenuity, instinct for what is elegant, a supple mind are their sole **hierarchy**, and often make of women of the people the equals of the very greatest ladies.

3   Mathilde suffered ceaselessly, feeling herself born to enjoy all delicacies and all luxuries. She was distressed at the poverty of her dwelling, at the bareness of the walls, at the shabby chairs, the ugliness of the curtains. All those things, of which another woman of her rank would never even have been conscious, tortured her and made her angry. The sight of the little Breton peasant who did her humble housework aroused in her despairing regrets and bewildering dreams. She thought of silent antechambers hung with Oriental tapestry, illumined by tall bronze candelabra, and of two great footmen in knee breeches who sleep in the big armchairs, made drowsy by the oppressive heat of the stove. She thought of long reception halls hung with ancient silk, of the dainty cabinets containing priceless curiosities and of the little coquettish perfumed reception rooms made for chatting at five o'clock with

Julie Daydreaming by Berthe Morisot, 1894

---

1. **dowry** money or property given to a man from the family of a woman in exchange for her becoming his bride

intimate friends, with men famous and sought after, whom all women envy and whose attention they all desire.

4 When she sat down to dinner, before the round table covered with a tablecloth in use three days, opposite her husband, who uncovered the soup tureen and declared with a delighted air, "Ah, the good soup! I don't know anything better than that," she thought of dainty dinners, of shining silverware, of tapestry that peopled the walls with ancient personages and with strange birds flying in the midst of a fairy forest; and she thought of delicious dishes served on marvelous plates and of the whispered gallantries to which you listen with a sphinxlike smile while you are eating the pink meat of a trout or the wings of a quail.

5 She had no gowns, no jewels, nothing. And she loved nothing but that. She felt made for that. She would have liked so much to please, to be envied, to be charming, to be sought after.

6 She had a friend, a former schoolmate at the convent, who was rich, and whom she did not like to go to see any more because she felt so sad when she came home.

7 But one evening her husband reached home with a triumphant air and holding a large envelope in his hand.

8 "There," said he, "there is something for you."

9 She tore the paper quickly and drew out a printed card which bore these words:

10 *The Minister of Public Instruction and Madame Georges Ramponneau
    request the honor of M. and Madame Loisel's company
    at the palace of the Ministry on Monday evening, January 18th.*

11 Instead of being delighted, as her husband had hoped, she threw the invitation on the table **crossly**, muttering:

12 "What do you wish me to do with that?"

13 "Why, my dear, I thought you would be glad. You never go out, and this is such a fine opportunity. I had great trouble to get it. Everyone wants to go; it is very select, and they are not giving many invitations to clerks. The whole official world will be there."

14 She looked at him with an irritated glance and said impatiently:

15 "And what do you wish me to put on my back?"

16 He had not thought of that. He stammered:

17 "Why, the gown you go to the theatre in. It looks very well to me."

18 He stopped, distracted, seeing that his wife was weeping. Two great tears ran slowly from the corners of her eyes toward the corners of her mouth.

19 "What's the matter? What's the matter?" he answered.

20 By a violent effort she conquered her grief and replied in a calm voice, while she wiped her wet cheeks:

21 "Nothing. Only I have no gown, and, therefore, I can't go to this ball. Give your card to some colleague whose wife is better equipped than I am."

22 He was in despair. He resumed:

23 "Come, let us see, Mathilde. How much would it cost, a suitable gown, which you could use on other occasions—something very simple?"

24 She reflected several seconds, making her calculations and wondering also what sum she could ask without drawing on herself an immediate refusal and a frightened exclamation from the economical clerk.

25 Finally she replied hesitating:

26 "I don't know exactly, but I think I could manage it with four hundred francs."

27 He grew a little pale, because he was laying aside just that amount to buy a gun and treat himself to a little shooting next summer on the plain of Nanterre, with several friends who went to shoot larks there of a Sunday.

28 But he said:

29 "Very well. I will give you four hundred francs. And try to have a pretty gown."

30 The day of the ball drew near and Madame Loisel seemed sad, uneasy, anxious. Her frock was ready, however. Her husband said to her one evening:

31 "What is the matter? Come, you have seemed very queer these last three days."

32 And she answered:

NOTES

33 "It annoys me not to have a single piece of jewelry, not a single ornament, nothing to put on. I shall look poverty-stricken. I would almost rather not go at all."

34 "You might wear natural flowers," said her husband. "They're very stylish at this time of year. For ten francs you can get two or three magnificent roses."

35 She was not convinced.

36 "No; there's nothing more humiliating than to look poor among other women who are rich."

37 "How stupid you are!" her husband cried. "Go look up your friend, Madame Forestier, and ask her to lend you some jewels. You're intimate enough with her to do that."

38 She uttered a cry of joy:

39 "True! I never thought of it."

40 The next day she went to her friend and told her of her distress.

41 Madame Forestier went to a wardrobe with a mirror, took out a large jewel box, brought it back, opened it and said to Madame Loisel:

42 "Choose, my dear."

43 She saw first some bracelets, then a pearl necklace, then a Venetian gold cross set with precious stones, of admirable workmanship. She tried on the ornaments before the mirror, hesitated and could not make up her mind to part with them, to give them back. She kept asking:

44 "Haven't you anymore?"

45 "Why, yes. Look further; I don't know what you like."

46 Suddenly she discovered, in a black satin box, a superb diamond necklace, and her heart throbbed with an immoderate desire. Her hands trembled as she took it. She fastened it round her throat, outside her high-necked waist, and was lost in ecstasy at her reflection in the mirror.

47 Then she asked, hesitating, filled with anxious doubt:

48 "Will you lend me this, only this?"

49 "Why, yes, certainly."

50   She threw her arms round her friend's neck, kissed her passionately, then fled with her treasure.

51   The night of the ball arrived. Madame Loisel was a great success. She was prettier than any other woman present, elegant, graceful, smiling and wild with joy. All the men looked at her, asked her name, sought to be introduced. All the attaches of the Cabinet wished to waltz with her. She was remarked by the minister himself.

52   She danced with **rapture**, with passion, intoxicated by pleasure, forgetting all in the triumph of her beauty, in the glory of her success, in a sort of cloud of happiness comprised of all this homage, admiration, these awakened desires and of that sense of triumph which is so sweet to woman's heart.

53   She left the ball about four o'clock in the morning. Her husband had been sleeping since midnight in a little deserted anteroom with three other gentlemen whose wives were enjoying the ball.

54   He threw over her shoulders the wraps he had brought, the modest wraps of common life, the poverty of which contrasted with the elegance of the ball dress. She felt this and wished to escape so as not to be remarked by the other women, who were enveloping themselves in costly furs.

55   Loisel held her back, saying: "Wait a bit. You will catch cold outside. I will call a cab."

56   But she did not listen to him and rapidly descended the stairs. When they reached the street they could not find a carriage and began to look for one, shouting after the cabmen passing at a distance.

57   They went toward the Seine in despair, shivering with cold. At last they found on the quay one of those ancient night cabs which, as though they were ashamed to show their shabbiness during the day, are never seen round Paris until after dark.

58   It took them to their dwelling in the Rue des Martyrs, and sadly they mounted the stairs to their flat. All was ended for her. As to him, he reflected that he must be at the ministry at ten o'clock that morning.

59   She removed her wraps before the glass so as to see herself once more in all her glory. But suddenly she uttered a cry. She no longer had the necklace around her neck!

60   "What is the matter with you?" demanded her husband, already half undressed.

Skill:
Theme

Madame Loisel is ashamed that she doesn't have a fur coat. She rushes away but can't find a carriage, which perhaps contributes to the loss of the necklace. These events suggest a possible theme: too much pride can lead to disaster.

Copyright © BookheadEd Learning, LLC

61 She turned distractedly toward him.

62 "I have—I have—I've lost Madame Forestier's necklace," she cried.

63 He stood up, bewildered.

64 "What!—how? Impossible!"

65 They looked among the folds of her skirt, of her cloak, in her pockets, everywhere, but did not find it.

66 "You're sure you had it on when you left the ball?" he asked.

67 "Yes, I felt it in the vestibule of the minister's house."

68 "But if you had lost it in the street we should have heard it fall. It must be in the cab."

69 "Yes, probably. Did you take his number?"

70 "No. And you—didn't you notice it?"

71 "No."

72 They looked, thunderstruck, at each other. At last Loisel put on his clothes.

73 "I shall go back on foot," said he, "over the whole route, to see whether I can find it."

74 He went out. She sat waiting on a chair in her ball dress, without strength to go to bed, overwhelmed, without any fire, without a thought.

75 Her husband returned about seven o'clock. He had found nothing.

76 He went to police headquarters, to the newspaper offices to offer a reward; he went to the cab companies—everywhere, in fact, whither he was urged by the least spark of hope.

77 She waited all day, in the same condition of mad fear before this terrible calamity.

78 Loisel returned at night with a hollow, pale face. He had discovered nothing.

79 "You must write to your friend," said he, "that you have broken the clasp of her necklace and that you are having it mended. That will give us time to turn round."

NOTES

80 She wrote at his **dictation**.

81 At the end of a week they had lost all hope. Loisel, who had aged five years, declared:

82 "We must consider how to replace that ornament."

83 The next day they took the box that had contained it and went to the jeweler whose name was found within. He consulted his books.

84 "It was not I, madame, who sold that necklace; I must simply have furnished the case."

85 Then they went from jeweler to jeweler, searching for a necklace like the other, trying to recall it, both sick with **chagrin** and grief.

86 They found, in a shop at the Palais Royal, a string of diamonds that seemed to them exactly like the one they had lost. It was worth forty thousand francs. They could have it for thirty-six.

87 So they begged the jeweler not to sell it for three days yet. And they made a bargain that he should buy it back for thirty-four thousand francs, in case they should find the lost necklace before the end of February.

88 Loisel possessed eighteen thousand francs which his father had left him. He would borrow the rest.

89 He did borrow, asking a thousand francs of one, five hundred of another, five louis here, three louis there. He gave notes, took up ruinous obligations, dealt with usurers and all the race of lenders. He compromised all the rest of his life, risked signing a note without even knowing whether he could meet it; and, frightened by the trouble yet to come, by the black misery that was about to fall upon him, by the prospect of all the physical privations and moral tortures that he was to suffer, he went to get the new necklace, laying upon the jeweler's counter thirty-six thousand francs.

90 When Madame Loisel took back the necklace Madame Forestier said to her with a chilly manner:

91 "You should have returned it sooner; I might have needed it."

92 She did not open the case, as her friend had so much feared. If she had detected the substitution, what would she have thought, what would she have said? Would she not have taken Madame Loisel for a thief?

Skill:
Theme

The loss of the necklace has a major impact on the rest of Loisel's life. He uses all his savings and borrows money to pay for a new necklace. This action refines the theme that trying to save face can lead to ruin.

Copyright © BookheadEd Learning, LLC

93   Thereafter Madame Loisel knew the horrible existence of the needy. She bore her part, however, with sudden heroism. That dreadful debt must be paid. She would pay it. They dismissed their servant; they changed their lodgings; they rented a garret under the roof.

94   She came to know what heavy housework meant and the odious cares of the kitchen. She washed the dishes, using her dainty fingers and rosy nails on greasy pots and pans. She washed the soiled linen, the shirts and the dishcloths, which she dried upon a line; she carried the slops down to the street every morning and carried up the water, stopping for breath at every landing. And dressed like a woman of the people, she went to the fruiterer, the grocer, the butcher, a basket on her arm, bargaining, meeting with **impertinence**, defending her miserable money, sou by sou.

95   Every month they had to meet some notes, renew others, obtain more time.

96   Her husband worked evenings, making up a tradesman's accounts, and late at night he often copied manuscript for five sous a page.

97   This life lasted ten years.

98   At the end of ten years they had paid everything, everything, with the rates of usury and the accumulations of the compound interest.

99   Madame Loisel looked old now. She had become the woman of impoverished households—strong and hard and rough. With frowsy hair, skirts askew and red hands, she talked loud while washing the floor with great swishes of water. But sometimes, when her husband was at the office, she sat down near the window and she thought of that gay evening of long ago, of that ball where she had been so beautiful and so admired.

100   What would have happened if she had not lost that necklace? Who knows? Who knows? How strange and changeful is life! How small a thing is needed to make or ruin us!

101   But one Sunday, having gone to take a walk in the Champs Elysées to refresh herself after the labors of the week, she suddenly perceived a woman who was leading a child. It was Madame Forestier, still young, still beautiful, still charming.

102   Madame Loisel felt moved. Should she speak to her? Yes, certainly. And now that she had paid, she would tell her all about it. Why not?

103   She went up.

104 "Good-day, Jeanne."

105 The other, astonished to be familiarly addressed by this plain good-wife, did not recognize her at all and stammered:

106 "But—madame!—I do not know—You must have mistaken."

107 "No. I am Mathilde Loisel."

108 Her friend uttered a cry.

109 "Oh, my poor Mathilde! How you are changed!"

110 "Yes, I have had a pretty hard life, since I last saw you, and great poverty—and that because of you!"

111 "Of me! How so?"

112 "Do you remember that diamond necklace you lent me to wear at the ministerial ball?"

113 "Yes. Well?"

114 "Well, I lost it."

115 "What do you mean? You brought it back."

116 "I brought you back another exactly like it. And it has taken us ten years to pay for it. You can understand that it was not easy for us, for us who had nothing. At last it is ended, and I am very glad."

117 Madame Forestier had stopped.

118 "You say that you bought a necklace of diamonds to replace mine?"

119 "Yes. You never noticed it, then! They were very similar."

120 And she smiled with a joy that was at once proud and ingenuous.

121 Madame Forestier, deeply moved, took her hands.

122 "Oh, my poor Mathilde! Why, my necklace was paste! It was worth at most only five hundred francs!"

Please note that excerpts and passages in the StudySync® library and this workbook are intended as touchstones to generate interest in an author's work. The excerpts and passages do not substitute for the reading of entire texts, and StudySync® strongly recommends that students seek out and purchase the whole literary or informational work in order to experience it as the author intended. Links to online resellers are available in our digital library. In addition, complete works may be ordered through an authorized reseller by filling out and returning to StudySync® the order form enclosed in this workbook.

Reading & Writing
Companion

27

First Read

Read "The Necklace." After you read, complete the Think Questions below.

1. Why is Madame Loisel so unsatisfied with her life in the beginning of the story? Cite specific evidence from the text to support your answer.

2. How does Madame Loisel interact with Madame Forestier after seeing her for the first time in 10 years? Use evidence from the text to support your answer.

3. What motivates Madame Loisel throughout the story? Be sure to use specific examples from the text to support your answer.

4. Use context to determine the meaning of the word **chagrin** as it is used in "The Necklace." Write your definition of *chagrin* here and explain how you came to this meaning. Then, consult a print or online dictionary to check your definition.

5. Use context to determine the meaning of the word **rapture** as it is used in "The Necklace." Write your definition of *rapture* here and explain how you came to this meaning. Then, consult a print or online dictionary to check your definition.

 **Skill:**
Theme

Use the Checklist to analyze Theme in "The Necklace." Refer to the sample student annotations about Theme in the text.

••• CHECKLIST FOR THEME

In order to identify a theme or central idea of a text, note the following:

✓ the subject of the text and a theme that might be stated directly in the text

✓ details in the text that help to reveal theme

- • the title and chapter headings
- • details about the setting
- • the narrator's or speaker's tone
- • characters' thoughts, actions, and dialogue
- • the central conflict in a story's plot
- • the climax, or turning point in the story
- • the resolution of the conflict
- • shifts in characters, setting, or plot events

✓ specific details that shape and refine the theme

To determine a theme or central idea of a text and analyze in detail its development over the course of the text, including how it emerges and is shaped and refined by specific details, consider the following questions:

✓ What is a theme of the text? How and when does it emerge?

✓ What specific details shape and refine the theme?

✓ How does the theme develop over the course of the text?

Please note that excerpts and passages in the StudySync® library and this workbook are intended as touchstones to generate interest in an author's work. The excerpts and passages do not substitute for the reading of entire texts, and StudySync® strongly recommends that students seek out and purchase the whole literary or informational work in order to experience it as the author intended. Links to online resellers are available in our digital library. In addition, complete works may be ordered through an authorized reseller by filling out and returning to StudySync® the order form enclosed in this workbook.

Reading & Writing Companion **29**

Skill:
Theme

Reread paragraphs 97–100 of "The Necklace." Then, using the Checklist on the previous page, answer the multiple-choice questions below.

↻ YOUR TURN

1. This question has two parts. First, answer Part A. Then, answer Part B.

   Part A: Which of the following statements best summarizes Mathilde's realization in this passage?

   ○ A. Hard work can be rewarding.

   ○ B. People's characters are shaped by their conditions.

   ○ C. Age brings unwelcome physical changes.

   ○ D. Harsh realities put an end to daydreams.

   Part B: What detail about changes in Madame Loisel's appearance and behavior from paragraphs 97–100 BEST support the theme identified in Part A?

   ○ A. "Madame Loisel looked old now. She had become the woman of impoverished households—strong and hard and rough."

   ○ B. "How strange and changeful is life! How small a thing is needed to make or ruin us!"

   ○ C. "At the end of ten years they had paid everything, everything, with the rates of usury and the accumulations of the compound interest."

   ○ D. "This life lasted ten years."

Close Read

Reread "The Necklace." As you reread, complete the Skills Focus questions below. Then use your answers and annotations from the questions to help you complete the Write activity.

◎ SKILLS FOCUS

1. Identify a passage in the beginning of the story that shows how the author uses narration to develop Mathilde Loisel's character. Explain how the details provided through this narration make her character believable.

2. Identify a passage that shows how the loss of the necklace impacts the Loisels. Then analyze how these plot events, driven in part by the characters' own actions, influence the theme.

3. Identify the passages toward the end of the story where the author advances the plot and reveals its effects on Mathilde Loisel. Describe how these effects contribute to the story's theme.

4. Identify textual evidence that reveals a plot twist in the ending and analyze its impact on the story's ultimate message.

✎ WRITE

LITERARY ANALYSIS: At the end of this short story, readers discover along with Mathilde Loisel that she has labored for ten years, lost her beauty, and declined into poverty to replace what was actually a fake diamond necklace. What does this plot twist, as well as other plot details, suggest about the story's themes? Write a thoughtful response supported by textual evidence and original commentary.

Please note that excerpts and passages in the StudySync® library and this workbook are intended as touchstones to generate interest in an author's work. The excerpts and passages do not substitute for the reading of entire texts, and StudySync® strongly recommends that students seek out and purchase the whole literary or informational work in order to experience it as the author intended. Links to online resellers are available in our digital library. In addition, complete works may be ordered through an authorized reseller by filling out and returning to StudySync® the order form enclosed in this workbook.

Reading & Writing
Companion

31

Metamorphoses
(Jupiter, Lycaon)

POETRY
Ovid
8 CE

Introduction

Ovid (43 BCE – 17 CE) was a Latin poet most famous today for his collection of myths and legends, *Metamorphoses*, originally written in hexameter verse—the standard in classical Greek and Latin literature. For reasons that remain uncertain, Ovid was banished from Rome by Emperor Augustus. Historians posit that his early love poems, which were considered immoral and against the sanctity of marriage, may have led to his exile. This excerpt details the reaction of Jupiter (Zeus in Greek mythology) to the degradation of humanity—in particular, to the contemptuous behavior of Lycaon, the king of Arcadia.

"Now I must destroy the human race, wherever Nereus sounds, throughout the world."

Book I: 177–198 Jupiter threatens to destroy humankind

1   When the gods had taken their seats in the marble council chamber their king, sitting high above them, leaning on his ivory sceptre, shook his **formidable** mane three times and then a fourth, disturbing the earth, sea and stars. Then he opened his lips in **indignation** and spoke. 'I was not more troubled than I am now concerning the world's sovereignty than when each of the snake-footed giants prepared to throw his hundred arms around the imprisoned sky. Though they were fierce enemies, still their attack came in one body and from one source. Now I must destroy the human race, wherever Nereus sounds, throughout the world. I swear it by the infernal streams, that glide below the earth through the Stygian groves[1]. All means should first be tried, but the incurable flesh must be excised by the knife, so that the healthy part is not infected. Mine are the demigods, the wild spirits, nymphs, fauns and satyrs, and sylvan deities of the hills. Since we have not yet thought them worth a place in heaven let us at least allow them to live in safety in the lands we have given them. Perhaps you gods believe they will be safe, even when Lycaon, known for his savagery, plays tricks against me, who holds the thunderbolt, and reigns over you.'

Book I: 199–243 Lycaon is turned into a wolf

2   All the gods murmured aloud and, zealously and eagerly, demanded punishment of the man who **committed** such actions. When the impious band of conspirators were burning to drown the name of Rome in Caesar's blood, the human race was suddenly terrified by fear of just such a disaster, and the whole world shuddered with horror. Your subjects' loyalty is no less pleasing to you, Augustus, than theirs was to Jupiter. After he had checked their murmuring with voice and gesture, they were all silent. When the noise had **subsided**, quieted by his royal authority, Jupiter again broke the silence with these words: 'Have no fear, he has indeed been punished, but I will tell you his crime, and what the penalty was. News of these evil times had

---

1. **Stygian groves** trees along the mythical river Styx, said to form the boundary between the worlds of the living and the dead

NOTES

reached my ears. Hoping it false I left Olympus's heights, and travelled the earth, a god in human form. It would take too long to tell what wickedness I found everywhere. Those rumours were even milder than the truth. I had crossed Maenala, those mountains bristling with wild beasts' lairs, Cyllene, and the pinewoods of chill Lycaeus. Then, as the last shadows gave way to night, I entered the inhospitable house of the Arcadian king. I gave them signs that a god had come, and the people began to worship me. At first Lycaon ridiculed their piety, then exclaimed 'I will prove by a straightforward test whether he is a god or a mortal. The truth will not be in doubt.' He planned to destroy me in the depths of sleep, unexpectedly, by night. That is how he resolved to prove the truth. Not satisfied with this he took a hostage sent by the Molossi[2], opened his throat with a knife, and made some of the still warm limbs **tender** in seething water, roasting others in the fire. No sooner were these placed on the table than I brought the roof down on the household gods, with my avenging flames, those gods worthy of such a master. He himself ran in terror, and reaching the silent fields howled aloud, frustrated of speech. Foaming at the mouth, and greedy as ever for killing, he turned against the sheep, still delighting in blood. His clothes became bristling hair, his arms became legs. He was a wolf, but kept some vestige of his former shape. There were the same grey hairs, the same violent face, the same glittering eyes, the same savage image. One house has fallen, but others deserve to also. Wherever the earth extends the avenging furies rule. You would think men were sworn to crime! Let them all pay the penalty they deserve, and quickly. That is my intent.'

✎ WRITE

PERSONAL RESPONSE: In the excerpt from Ovid's *Metamorphoses*, Jupiter turns Lycaon into a wolf. Why do you think Jupiter chose to turn him into this particular animal? What is the significance of the wolf? How do you think it represents Lycaon's nature? Evaluate and analyze the significance of this transformation based on the excerpt and what you know about Lycaon.

2. **Molossi** an ancient Greek tribe

Braving the Wilderness:
The Quest for True Belonging and the Courage to Stand Alone

INFORMATIONAL TEXT
Brené Brown
2017

Introduction

Brené Brown (b. 1965) is a writer and teacher, as well as the CEO of Brave Leaders, Inc., which teaches team-building to organizations. She is best known for her viral TED-Talk, "The Power of Vulnerability." She is also the author of *Braving the Wilderness: The Quest for True Belonging and the Courage to Stand Alone,* which focuses on empathy, courage, shame and vulnerability. In this excerpt, the author reflects on trying out for her high school's drill team, using the experience to teach valuable lessons about success, failure and belonging.

"I practiced so much that I could do that routine in my sleep."

NOTES

1   When we moved back to Houston at the very end of eighth grade there was, thankfully, just enough time to try out for the high school drill team, called the Bearkadettes. This was to be my everything. In a house that was increasingly filled with the muffled sounds of my parents arguing, heard through the walls of my bedroom, that drill team was salvation. Just picture it: lines of girls in white-fringed blue satin vests and short skirts, all of them wearing uniform wigs, white cowboy boots, small white cowboy hats, and bright red lipstick, strutting into high school football stadiums filled with crowds afraid to leave their seats during halftime lest they miss the high kicks and perfectly **choreographed** routines. This was my way out, my new, pretty, impeccably ordered **refuge**.

2   Eight years of ballet was plenty to get me through the task of learning the routine, and a two-week liquid diet got me through the brutal weigh-in. All of the girls swore by the cabbage soup and water diet. It's hard to think of letting a twelve-year-old go on a liquid diet, but for some reason it seemed normal.

3   To this day, I'm not sure I've ever wanted anything in my life more than I wanted a place on this drill team. The perfection, **precision**, and beauty of it would not only offset the growing turmoil at home, but also deliver the holy grail of belonging. I would have a "big sis" and she would decorate my locker. We'd have sleepovers and date football players. For a kid who had seen *Grease* forty-five times, I knew this was the beginning of a high school experience that included sudden, spontaneous sing-alongs and the 1980s version of sock hops[1].

4   And most of all, I would be part of something that literally did everything together in lockstep. A Bearkadette was belonging personified.

5   I didn't really have any friends yet, so I was on my own for tryouts. The routine was easy to learn—a jazzy number performed to a big band version of "Swanee" (you know, the "how I love ya, how I love ya" one). There was a lot

---

1. **sock hops** events popular in the 1950s at which teenagers danced in their socks and socialized

NOTES

of sliding with jazz hands and an entire section of high kicks. I could kick higher than all of the girls except one dancer named LeeAnne. I practiced so much that I could do that routine in my sleep. I still remember parts of it today.

6   Tryout day was terrifying, and I'm not sure if it was my nerves or the starvation diet, but I was lightheaded when I woke up, and I stayed that way after my mom dropped me off at school. Now, as a mother of a teen and a tween, it's a little hard to think of how I had to walk in by myself, surrounded by groups of girls who were piling out of cars and running in together, holding hands. But I soon realized I had a bigger problem than walking in alone.

7   All of the girls—and I mean *all* of the girls—were made up from head to toe. Some were wearing blue satin shorts and gold shirts, and others had blue and gold tank tops with little white skirts. There was every iteration of blue and gold bows that you could imagine. And they were all in full makeup. I had on no makeup, and I was wearing gray cotton shorts over a black leotard. No one had told me that you were supposed to get decked out in school colors. Everyone looked so bright and shiny. I looked like the sad girl whose parents fight a lot.

8   I made the weigh-in with six pounds to spare. Even so, the sight of girls stepping off the scale and running into the locker room weeping traumatized me.

9   We wore numbers safety-pinned to our shirts and danced in groups of five or six. Lightheaded or not, I nailed the routine. I felt pretty confident when my mom picked me up and I went home to wait it out. They would post the numbers later in the evening. Those hours in between moved in slow motion.

10 Finally, at five after six, we pulled into the parking lot of my soon-to-be high school. My entire family—mom, dad, brother and sisters—was in the car. I was going to check my number and then we were headed to San Antonio to visit my grandparents. I walked up to the poster board hanging on the outside of the gym door. Standing next to me was one of the girls from the tryout group. She was the brightest and shiniest of all the girls. And on top of all that, her name was Kris. Yes, she even had one of those **coveted** girl-body names that we all wanted.

11 The list was in numeric order. If your number was there, you'd made the team. If your number wasn't there, you were out. I was number 62. My eye went straight for the 60s: 59, 61, 64, 65. I looked again. I just couldn't process it. I thought if I stared hard enough and the universe knew how much was on the line, the number might magically appear. I was ripped out of my **negotiation** with the universe by Kris's screaming. She was jumping up and down, and before I could makes sense of what was happening, her dad had jumped out

Please note that excerpts and passages in the StudySync® library and this workbook are intended as touchstones to generate interest in an author's work. The excerpts and passages do not substitute for the reading of entire texts, and StudySync® strongly recommends that students seek out and purchase the whole literary or informational work in order to experience it as the author intended. Links to online resellers are available in our digital library. In addition, complete works may be ordered through an authorized reseller by filling out and returning to StudySync® the order form enclosed in this workbook.

Reading & Writing
Companion

37

of the car, run up to her, grabbed her, and twirled her around, just like in the movies. I would later hear through the grapevine that I was a solid dancer but not really Bearkadette material. No bows. No shine. No group. No friends. Nowhere to belong.

12   *I was alone*. And it felt devastating.

13   I walked back to our station wagon and got in the backseat, and my dad drove away. My parents didn't say one word. Not a single word. The silence cut into me like a knife to the heart. They were ashamed of me and for me. My dad had been captain of the football team. My mom had been head of her drill team. I was nothing. My parents, especially my father, valued being cool and fitting in above all else. I was not cool. I didn't fit in.

14   And now, for the first time, I didn't belong to my family either.

15   My drill team story is one that's easy to dismiss as unimportant in the larger scheme of what's going on in the world today. (I can already see the #firstworldproblems hashtag.) But let me tell you what it means to me. I don't know if this was true or it was the story I told myself in that silence, but that became the day I no longer belonged in my family—the most primal and important of all our social groups. Had my parents consoled me or told me I was brave for trying—or, better yet and what I really wanted in that moment, had they taken my side and told me how terrible it was and how I deserved to be picked—this story wouldn't be one that defined my life and shaped its trajectory. But it did.

Excerpted from *Braving the Wilderness: The Quest for True Belonging and the Courage to Stand Alone* by Brené Brown, published by Random House.

 WRITE

NARRATIVE: In this text, the author, Brené Brown, describes an event from her teenage years that forever damaged her relationship with her parents. What event from your life so far might you look back on years from now as having had a lasting impact on your personality, your relationships, or your outlook—for better or for worse? Describe the event in a personal narrative that, like Brown's text, includes a clear setting, a sequence of events, descriptive sensory details, and a reflection on the experience's significance.

St. Lucy's Home for Girls Raised by Wolves

FICTION
Karen Russell
2006

Introduction

Born and raised in Miami, Florida, Karen Russell (b. 1981) is a bestselling author known for her distinctive, magical realist style. Her first novel, *Swamplandia!*, was a finalist for the Pulitzer Prize in 2012. The short story presented here, "St. Lucy's Home for Girls Raised by Wolves," was published in Russell's debut 2006 collection of the same name. In this fantastical tale, a pack of girls descended from werewolves attends a boarding school to learn how to behave like regular humans.

"Our mothers and fathers were werewolves."

NOTES

1 Stage 1: The initial period is one in which everything is new, exciting, and interesting for your students. It is fun for your students to explore their new environment.
—from The Jesuit[1] Handbook on Lycanthropic[2] Culture Shock.

. . .

2 At first, our pack was all hair and snarl and floor-thumping joy. We forgot the barked cautions of our mothers and fathers, all the promises we'd made to be civilized and ladylike, couth and kempt. We tore through the **austere** rooms, overturning dresser drawers, pawing through the neat piles of the Stage 3 girls' starched underwear, smashing light bulbs with our bare fists. Things felt less foreign in the dark. The dim bedroom was windowless and odorless. We remedied this by spraying exuberant yellow streams all over the bunks. We jumped from bunk to bunk, spraying. We nosed each other midair, our bodies buckling in kinetic laughter. The nuns watched us from the corner of the bedroom, their tiny faces pinched with displeasure.

Skill: Allusion

The nuns remind me of the gods in Ovid's story. They have power and authority over the wolf-girls like the gods have over the human race. Similarly, the nuns judge the wolf-girls' behavior and think they are savages from the "backwoods" who need to be controlled and civilized.

3 "Ay caramba," Sister Maria de la Guardia sighed. "Que barbaridad!" She made the Sign of the Cross. Sister Maria came to St. Lucy's from a halfway home in Copacabana. In Copacabana, the girls are fat and languid and eat pink slivers of guava right out of your hand. Even at Stage 1, their pelts are silky, sun-bleached to near invisibility. Our pack was hirsute and sinewy and mostly brunette. We had terrible posture. We went knuckling along the wooden floor on the calloused pads of our fists, baring row after row of tiny, wood-rotted teeth. Sister Josephine sucked in her breath. She removed a yellow wheel of floss from under her robes, looping it like a miniature lasso.

4 "The girls at our facility are backwoods," Sister Josephine whispered to Sister Maria de la Guardia with a beatific smile. "You must be patient with them." I clamped down on her ankle, straining to close my jaws around the woolly XXL sock. Sister Josephine tasted like sweat and freckles. She smelled easy to kill.

---

1. **Jesuit** a member of a scholarly order of the Roman Catholic Church
2. **Lycanthropic** pertaining to someone who suffers from lycanthropy, the belief that he or she is a wolf, especially a werewolf

5   We'd arrived at St. Lucy's that morning, part of a pack fifteen-strong. We were accompanied by a mousy, nervous-smelling social worker; the baby-faced deacon; Bartholomew, the blue wolfhound; and four burly woodsmen. The deacon handed out some stale cupcakes and said a quick prayer. Then he led us through the woods. We ran past the wild apiary, past the felled oaks, until we could see the white steeple of St. Lucy's rising out of the forest. We stopped short at the edge of a muddy lake. Then the deacon took our brothers. Bartholomew helped him to herd the boys up the ramp of a small ferry. We girls ran along the shore, tearing at our new jumpers in a plaid agitation. Our brothers stood on the deck, looking small and confused.

6   Our mothers and fathers were werewolves. They lived an outsider's existence in caves at the edge of the forest, threatened by frost and pitchforks. They had been **ostracized** by the local farmers for eating their silled fruit pies and terrorizing the heifers. They had ostracized the local wolves by having sometimes-thumbs, and regrets, and human children. (Their condition skips a generation.) Our pack grew up in a green purgatory. We couldn't keep up with the purebred wolves, but we never stopped crawling. We spoke a slab-tongued pidgin in the cave, inflected with frequent howls. Our parents wanted something better for us; they wanted us to get braces, use towels, be fully bilingual. When the nuns showed up, our parents couldn't refuse their offer. The nuns, they said, would make us naturalized citizens of human society. We would go to St. Lucy's to study a better culture. We didn't know at the time that our parents were sending us away for good. Neither did they.

7   That first afternoon, the nuns gave us free rein of the grounds. Everything was new, exciting, and interesting. A low granite wall surrounded St. Lucy's, the blue woods humming for miles behind it. There was a stone fountain full of delectable birds. There was a statue of St. Lucy. Her marble skin was colder than our mother's nose, her pupil-less eyes rolled heavenward. Doomed squirrels gamboled around her stony toes. Our diminished pack threw back our heads in a celebratory howl—an exultant and terrible noise, even without a chorus of wolf brothers in the background. There were holes everywhere!

8   We supplemented these holes by digging some of our own. We interred sticks, and our itchy new jumpers, and the bones of the friendly, unfortunate squirrels. Our noses ached beneath an invisible assault. Everything was smudged with a human odor: baking bread, petrol, the nuns' faint woman-smell sweating out beneath a dark perfume of tallow and incense. We smelled one another, too, with the same astounded fascination. Our own scent had become foreign in this strange place.

9   We had just sprawled out in the sun for an afternoon nap, yawning into the warm dirt, when the nuns reappeared. They **conferred** in the shadow of the juniper tree, whispering and pointing. Then they started towards us. The oldest sister had spent the past hour twitching in her sleep, dreaming of fatty and infirm elk. (The pack used to dream the same dreams back then, as naturally as we drank the same water and slept on the same red scree.)

When our oldest sister saw the nuns approaching, she instinctively bristled. It was an improvised bristle, given her new, human limitations. She took clumps of her scraggly, nut-brown hair and held it straight out from her head.

10   Sister Maria gave her a brave smile.

11   "And what is your name?" she asked.

12   The oldest sister howled something awful and inarticulable, a distillate of hurt and panic, half-forgotten hunts and eclipsed moons. Sister Maria nodded and scribbled on a yellow legal pad. She slapped on a name tag: HELLO, MY NAME IS! "Jeanette it is."

13   The rest of the pack ran in a loose, uncertain circle, torn between our instinct to help her and our new fear. We sensed some subtler danger afoot, written in a language we didn't understand.

14   Our littlest sister had the quickest reflexes. She used her hands to flatten her ears to the side of her head. She backed towards the far corner of the garden, snarling in the most menacing register that an eight-year-old wolf-girl can muster. Then she ran. It took them two hours to pin her down and tag her: HELLO, MY NAME IS MIRABELLA!

15   "Stage 1," Sister Maria sighed, taking careful aim with her tranquilizer dart. "It can be a little overstimulating."

. . .

16   Stage 2: After a time, your students realize that they must work to adjust to the new culture. This work may be stressful and students may experience a strong sense of dislocation. They may miss certain foods. They may spend a lot of time daydreaming during this period. Many students feel isolated, irritated, bewildered, depressed, or generally uncomfortable.

. . .

17   Those were the days when we dreamed of rivers and meat. The full-moon nights were the worst! Worse than cold toilet seats and boiled tomatoes, worse than trying to will our tongues to curl around our false new names. We would snarl at one another for no reason. I remember how disorienting it was to look down and see two square-toed shoes instead of my own four feet. Keep your mouth shut, I repeated during our walking drills, staring straight ahead. Keep your shoes on your feet. Mouth shut, shoes on feet. Do not chew on your new penny loafers. Do not. I stumbled around in a daze, my mouth black with shoe polish. The whole pack was irritated, bewildered, depressed. We were all uncomfortable, and between languages. We had never wanted to run away so badly in our lives; but who did we have to run back to? Only the curled black grimace of the mother. Only the father, holding

his tawny head between his paws. Could we betray our parents by going back to them? After they'd given us the choicest part of the woodchuck, loved us at our hairless worst, nosed us across the ice floes and abandoned us at St. Lucy's for our own betterment?

18 Physically, we were all easily capable of clearing the low stone walls. Sister Josephine left the wooden gates wide open. They unslatted the windows at night so that long fingers of moonlight beckoned us from the woods. But we knew we couldn't return to the woods; not till we were civilized, not if we didn't want to break the mother's heart. It all felt like a sly, human taunt.

19 It was impossible to make the blank, chilly bedroom feel like home. In the beginning, we drank gallons of bathwater as part of a collaborative effort to mark our territory. We puddled up the yellow carpet of old newspapers. But later, when we returned to the bedroom, we were dismayed to find all trace of the pack musk had vanished. Someone was coming in and erasing us. We sprayed and sprayed every morning; and every night, we returned to the same ammonia eradication. We couldn't make our scent stick here; it made us feel invisible. Eventually we gave up. Still, the pack seemed to be adjusting on the same timetable. The advanced girls could already alternate between two speeds: "slouch" and "amble." Almost everybody was fully bipedal.

20 Almost.

21 The pack was worried about Mirabella.

22 Mirabella would rip foamy chunks out of the church pews and replace them with ham bones and girl dander. She loved to roam the grounds wagging her invisible tail. (We all had a hard time giving that up. When we got excited, we would fall to the ground and start pumping our backsides. Back in those days we could pump at rabbity velocities. "Que horror!" Sister Maria frowned, looking more than a little jealous.) We'd give her scolding pinches. "Mirabella," we hissed, imitating the nuns. "No." Mirabella cocked her ears at us, hurt and confused.

23 Still, some things remained the same. The main commandment of wolf life is Know Your Place, and that translated perfectly. Being around other humans had awakened a slavish-dog affection in us. An **abasing**, belly-to-the-ground desire to please. As soon as we realized that someone higher up in the food chain was watching us, we wanted only to be pleasing in their sight. Mouth shut, I repeated, shoes on feet. But if Mirabella had this latent instinct, the nuns couldn't figure out how to activate it. She'd go bounding around, gleefully spraying on their gilded statue of St. Lucy, mad-scratching at the virulent fleas that survived all of their powders and baths. At Sister Maria's tearful insistence, she'd stand upright for roll call, her knobby, oddly muscled legs quivering from the effort. Then she'd collapse right back to the ground with an ecstatic oomph! She was still loping around on all fours (which the nuns had taught us to see looked unnatural and ridiculous—we could barely

Please note that excerpts and passages in the StudySync® library and this workbook are intended as touchstones to generate interest in an author's work. The excerpts and passages do not substitute for the reading of entire texts, and StudySync® strongly recommends that students seek out and purchase the whole literary or informational work in order to experience it as the author intended. Links to online resellers are available in our digital library. In addition, complete works may be ordered through an authorized reseller by filling out and returning to StudySync® the order form enclosed in this workbook.

Reading & Writing Companion

43

NOTES

believe it now, the shame of it, that we used to **locomote** like that!), her fists blue-white from the strain. As if she were holding a secret tight to the ground. Sister Maria de la Guardia would sigh every time she saw her. "Caramba!" She'd sit down with Mirabella and pry her fingers apart. "You see?" she'd say softly, again and again. "What are you holding on to? Nothing, little one. Nothing."

24 Then she would sing out the standard chorus, "Why can't you be more like your sister Jeanette?"

25 The pack hated Jeanette. She was the most successful of us, the one furthest removed from her origins. Her real name was GWARR!, but she wouldn't respond to this anymore. Jeanette spiffed her penny loafers until her very shoes seemed to gloat. (Linguists have since traced the colloquial origins of "goody two-shoes" back to our facilities.) She could even growl out a demonic-sounding precursor to "Pleased to meet you." She'd delicately extend her former paws to visitors, wearing white kid gloves.

26 "Our little wolf, disguised in sheep's clothing!" Sister Ignatius liked to joke with the visiting deacons, and Jeanette would surprise everyone by laughing along with them, a harsh, inhuman, barking sound. Her hearing was still twig-snap sharp. Jeanette was the first among us to apologize; to drink apple juice out of a sippy cup; to quit eyeballing the cleric's jugular in a disconcerting fashion. She curled her lips back into a cousin of a smile as the traveling barber cut her pelt into bangs. Then she swept her coarse black curls under the rug. When we entered a room, our nostrils flared beneath the new odors: onion and bleach, candle wax, the turnipy smell of unwashed bodies. Not Jeanette. Jeanette smiled and pretended like she couldn't smell a thing.

27 I was one of the good girls. Not great and not terrible, solidly middle of the pack. But I had an ear for languages, and I could read before I could adequately wash myself. I probably could have vied with Jeanette for the number one spot, but I'd seen what happened if you gave in to your natural aptitudes. This wasn't like the woods, where you had to be your fastest and your strongest and your bravest self. Different sorts of calculations were required to survive at the home.

28 The pack hated Jeanette, but we hated Mirabella more. We began to avoid her, but sometimes she'd surprise us, curled up beneath the beds or gnawing on a scapula in the garden. It was scary to be ambushed by your sister. I'd bristle and growl, the way that I'd begun to snarl at my own reflection as if it were a stranger.

29 "Whatever will become of Mirabella?" we asked, gulping back our own fear. We'd heard rumors about former wolf-girls who never adapted to their new culture. It was assumed that they were returned to our native country, the vanishing woods. We liked to speculate about this before bedtime, scaring ourselves with stories of catastrophic bliss. It was the disgrace, the failure that

we all guiltily hoped for in our hard beds. Twitching with the shadow question: *Whatever will become of me?*

30   We spent a lot of time daydreaming during this period. Even Jeanette. Sometimes I'd see her looking out at the woods in a vacant way. If you interrupted her in the midst of one of these reveries, she would lunge at you with an elder-sister ferocity, momentarily forgetting her human catechism. We liked her better then, startled back into being foamy old Jeanette.

31   In school, they showed us the St. Francis of Assisi slide show, again and again. Then the nuns would give us bags of bread. They never announced these things as a test; it was only much later that I realized that we were under constant examination. "Go feed the ducks," they urged us. "Go practice compassion for all God's creatures." *Don't pair me with Mirabella*, I prayed, *anybody but Mirabella*. "Claudette"—Sister Josephine beamed—"why don't you and Mirabella take some pumpernickel down to the ducks?"

32   "Ohhkaaythankyou," I said. (It took me a long time to say anything; first I had to translate it in my head from the Wolf.) It wasn't fair. They knew Mirabella couldn't make bread balls yet. She couldn't even undo the twist tie of the bag. She was sure to eat the birds; Mirabella didn't even try to curb her desire to kill things—and then who would get blamed for the dark spots of duck blood on our Peter Pan collars? Who would get penalized with negative Skill Points? Exactly.

33   As soon as we were beyond the wooden gates, I snatched the bread away from Mirabella and ran off to the duck pond on my own. Mirabella gave chase, nipping at my heels. She thought it was a game. "Stop it," I growled. I ran faster, but it was Stage 2 and I was still unsteady on my two feet. I fell sideways into a leaf pile, and then all I could see was my sister's blurry form, bounding towards me. In a moment, she was on top of me, barking the old word for tug-of-war. When she tried to steal the bread out of my hands, I whirled around and snarled at her, pushing my ears back from my head. I bit her shoulder, once, twice, the only language she would respond to. I used my new motor skills. I threw dirt, I threw stones. "Get away!" I screamed, long after she had made a cringing retreat into the shadows of the purple saplings. "Get away, get away!"

34   Much later, they found Mirabella wading in the shallows of a distant river, trying to strangle a mallard with her rosary beads. I was at the lake; I'd been sitting there for hours. Hunched in the long cattails, my yellow eyes flashing, shoving ragged hunks of bread into my mouth.

35   I don't know what they did to Mirabella. Me they separated from my sisters. They made me watch another slide show. This one showed images of former wolf-girls, the ones who had failed to be rehabilitated. Long-haired, sad-eyed women, limping after their former wolf packs in white tennis shoes and pleated culottes. A wolf-girl bank teller, her makeup smeared in

Please note that excerpts and passages in the StudySync® library and this workbook are intended as touchstones to generate interest in an author's work. The excerpts and passages do not substitute for the reading of entire texts, and StudySync® strongly recommends that students seek out and purchase the whole literary or informational work in order to experience it as the author intended. Links to online resellers are available in our digital library. In addition, complete works may be ordered through an authorized reseller by filling out and returning to StudySync® the order form enclosed in this workbook.

Reading & Writing Companion   45

oily rainbows, eating a raw steak on the deposit slips while her colleagues looked on in disgust. Our parents. The final slide was a bolded sentence in St. Lucy's prim script: DO YOU WANT TO END UP SHUNNED BY BOTH SPECIES?

36 After that, I spent less time with Mirabella. One night she came to me, holding her hand out. She was covered with splinters, keening a high, whining noise through her nostrils. Of course I understood what she wanted; I wasn't that far removed from our language (even though I was reading at a fifth-grade level, halfway into Jack London's *The Son of the Wolf*).

37 "Lick your own wounds," I said, not unkindly. It was what the nuns had instructed us to say; wound licking was not something you did in polite company. Etiquette was so confounding in this country. Still, looking at Mirabella—her fists balled together like small, white porcupines, her brows knitted in animal confusion—I felt a throb of compassion. *How can people live like they do?* I wondered. Then I congratulated myself. This was a Stage 3 thought.

. . .

38 Stage 3: It is common that students who start living in a new and different culture come to a point where they reject the host culture and withdraw into themselves. During this period, they make generalizations about the host culture and wonder how the people can live like they do. Your students may feel that their own culture's lifestyle and customs are far superior to those of the host country.

. . .

39 The nuns were worried about Mirabella, too. To correct a failing, you must first be aware of it as a failing. And there was Mirabella, shucking her plaid jumper in full view of the visiting cardinal. Mirabella, battling a raccoon under the dinner table while the rest of us took dainty bites of peas and borscht. Mirabella, doing belly flops into compost.

40 "You have to pull your weight around here," we overheard Sister Josephine saying one night. We paused below the vestry window and peered inside.

41 "Does Mirabella try to earn Skill Points by shelling walnuts and polishing Saint-in-the-Box? No. Does Mirabella even know how to say the word walnut? Has she learned how to say anything besides a sinful 'HraaaHA!' as she commits frottage against the organ pipes? No."

42 There was a long silence.

43 "Something must be done," Sister Ignatius said firmly. The other nuns nodded, a sea of thin, colorless lips and kettle-black brows. "Something must be done,"

NOTES

they intoned. That ominously passive construction; a something so awful that nobody wanted to assume responsibility for it.

44   I could have warned her. If we were back home, and Mirabella had come under attack by territorial beavers or snow-blind bears, I would have warned her. But the truth is that by Stage 3 I wanted her gone. Mirabella's inability to adapt was taking a visible toll. Her teeth were ground down to nubbins; her hair was falling out. She hated the spongy, long-dead foods we were served, and it showed—her ribs were poking through her uniform. Her bright eyes had dulled to a sour whiskey color. But you couldn't show Mirabella the slightest kindness anymore—she'd never leave you alone! You'd have to sit across from her at meals, shoving her away as she begged for your scraps. I slept fitfully during that period, unable to forget that Mirabella was living under my bed, gnawing on my loafers.

45   It was during Stage 3 that we met our first purebred girls. These were girls raised in captivity, volunteers from St. Lucy's School for Girls. The apple-cheeked fourth-grade class came to tutor us in playing. They had long golden braids or short, severe bobs. They had frilly-duvet names like Felicity and Beulah; and pert, bunny noses; and terrified smiles. We grinned back at them with genuine ferocity. It made us nervous to meet new humans. There were so many things that we could do wrong! And the rules here were different depending on which humans we were with: dancing or no dancing, checkers playing or no checkers playing, pumping or no pumping.

46   The purebred girls played checkers with us.

47   "These girl-girls sure is dumb," my sister Lavash panted to me between games. "I win it again! Five to none."

48   She was right. The purebred girls were making mistakes on purpose, in order to give us an advantage. "King me," I growled, out of turn. "I say king me!" and Felicity meekly complied. Beulah pretended not to mind when we got frustrated with the oblique, fussy movement from square to square and shredded the board to ribbons. I felt sorry for them. I wondered what it would be like to be bred in captivity, and always homesick for a dimly sensed forest, the trees you've never seen.

49   Jeanette was learning how to dance. On Holy Thursday, she mastered a rudimentary form of the Charleston. "Brava!" The nuns clapped. "Brava!"

50   Every Friday, the girls who had learned how to ride a bicycle celebrated by going on chaperoned trips into town. The purebred girls sold seven hundred rolls of gift-wrap paper and used the proceeds to buy us a yellow fleet of bicycles built for two. We'd ride the bicycles uphill, a sanctioned pumping, a grim-faced nun pedaling behind each one of us. "Congratulations!" the nuns would huff. "Being human is like riding this bicycle. Once you've learned how,

Please note that excerpts and passages in the StudySync® library and this workbook are intended as touchstones to generate interest in an author's work. The excerpts and passages do not substitute for the reading of entire texts, and StudySync® strongly recommends that students seek out and purchase the whole literary or informational work in order to experience it as the author intended. Links to online resellers are available in our digital library. In addition, complete works may be ordered through an authorized reseller by filling out and returning to StudySync® the order form enclosed in this workbook.

Reading & Writing Companion   47

you'll never forget." Mirabella would run after the bicycles, growling out our old names. HWRAA! GWARR! TRRRRRRR! We pedaled faster.

51 At this point, we'd had six weeks of lessons, and still nobody could do the Sausalito but Jeanette. The nuns decided we needed an inducement to dance. They announced that we would celebrate our successful rehabilitations with a Debutante Ball. There would be brothers, ferried over from the Home for Man-Boys Raised by Wolves. There would be a photographer from the Gazette Sophisticate. There would be a three-piece jazz band from West Toowoomba, and root beer in tiny plastic cups. The brothers! We'd almost forgotten about them. Our invisible tails went limp. I should have been excited; instead, I felt a low mad anger at the nuns. They knew we weren't ready to dance with the brothers; we weren't even ready to talk to them. Things had been so much simpler in the woods. That night I waited until my sisters were asleep. Then I slunk into the closet and practiced the Sausalito two-step in secret, a private mass of twitch and foam. Mouth shut—shoes on feet! Mouth shut—shoes on feet! Mouthshutmouthshut. . .

52 One night I came back early from the closet and stumbled on Jeanette. She was sitting in a patch of moonlight on the windowsill, reading from one of her library books. (She was the first of us to sign for her library card, too.) Her cheeks looked dewy.

53 "Why you cry?" I asked her, instinctively reaching over to lick Jeanette's cheek and catching myself in the nick of time.

54 Jeanette blew her nose into a nearby curtain. (Even her mistakes annoyed us—they were always so well intentioned.) She sniffled and pointed to a line in her book: "The lake-water was reinventing the forest and the white moon above it, and wolves lapped up the cold reflection of the sky." But none of the pack besides me could read yet, and I wasn't ready to claim a common language with Jeanette.

55 The following day, Jeanette golfed. The nuns set up a miniature putt-putt course in the garden. Sister Maria dug four sandtraps and got old Walter, the groundskeeper, to make a windmill out of a lawn mower engine. The eighteenth hole was what they called a "doozy," a minuscule crack in St. Lucy's marble dress. Jeanette got a hole in one.

56 On Sundays, the pretending felt almost as natural as nature. The chapel was our favorite place. Long before we could understand what the priest was saying, the music instructed us in how to feel. The choir director—aggressively perfumed Mrs. Valuchi, gold necklaces like pineapple rings around her neck—taught us more than the nuns ever did. She showed us how to pattern the old hunger into arias. Clouds moved behind the frosted oculus of the nave, glass shadows that reminded me of my mother. The mother, I'd think, struggling to conjure up a picture. A black shadow, running behind the watery screen of pines.

57   We sang at the chapel annexed to the home every morning. We understood that this was the humans' moon, the place for howling beyond purpose. Not for mating, not for hunting, not for fighting, not for anything but the sound itself. And we'd howl along with the choir, hurling every pitted thing within us at the stained glass. "Sotto voce[3]." The nuns would frown. But you could tell that they were pleased.

. . .

58   Stage 4: As a more thorough understanding of the host culture is acquired, your students will begin to feel more comfortable in their new environment. Your students feel more at home, and their self-confidence grows. Everything begins to make sense.

. . .

59   "Hey, Claudette," Jeanette growled to me on the day before the ball. "Have you noticed that everything's beginning to make sense?"

60   Before I could answer, Mirabella sprang out of the hall closet and snapped through Jeanette's homework binder. Pages and pages of words swirled around the stone corridor, like dead leaves off trees.

61   "What about you, Mirabella?" Jeanette asked politely, stooping to pick up her erasers. She was the only one of us who would still talk to Mirabella; she was high enough in the rankings that she could afford to talk to the scruggliest wolf-girl. "Has everything begun to make more sense, Mirabella?"

62   Mirabella let out a whimper. She scratched at us and scratched at us, raking her nails along our shins so hard that she drew blood. Then she rolled belly-up on the cold stone floor, squirming on a bed of spelling-bee worksheets. Above us, small pearls of light dotted the high, tinted window.

63   Jeanette frowned. "You are a late bloomer, Mirabella! Usually, everything's begun to make more sense by Month Twelve at the latest." I noticed that she stumbled on the word bloomer. HraaaHA! Jeanette could never fully shake our accent. She'd talk like that her whole life, I thought with a gloomy satisfaction, each word winced out like an apology for itself.

64   "Claudette, help me," she yelped. Mirabella had closed her jaws around Jeanette's bald ankle and was dragging her towards the closet. "Please. Help me to mop up Mirabella's mess."

---

3. **sotto voce** a musical directive that indicates something should be sung softly or under one's breath

65   I ignored her and continued down the hall. I had only four more hours to perfect the Sausalito. I was worried only about myself. By that stage, I was no longer certain of how the pack felt about anything.

66   At seven o'clock on the dot, Sister Ignatius blew her whistle and frog-marched us into the ball. The nuns had transformed the rectory into a very scary place. Purple and silver balloons started popping all around us. Black streamers swooped down from the eaves and got stuck in our hair like bats. A full yellow moon smirked outside the window. We were greeted by blasts of a saxophone, and fizzy pink drinks, and the brothers.

67   The brothers didn't smell like our brothers anymore. They smelled like pomade and cold, sterile sweat. They looked like little boys. Someone had washed behind their ears and made them wear suspendered dungarees. Kyle used to be a blustery alpha male, BTWWWR!, chewing through rattlesnakes, spooking badgers, snatching a live trout out of a grizzly's mouth. He stood by the punch bowl, looking pained and out of place.

68   "My stars!" I growled. "What lovely weather we've been having!"

69   "Yeees," Kyle growled back. "It is beginning to look a lot like Christmas." All around the room, boys and girls raised by wolves were having the same conversation. Actually, it had been an unseasonably warm and brown winter, and just that morning a freak hailstorm had sent Sister Josephina to an early grave. But we had only gotten up to Unit 7: Party Dialogue; we hadn't yet learned the vocabulary for Unit 12: How to Tactfully Acknowledge Disaster. Instead, we wore pink party hats and sucked olives on little sticks, inured to our own strangeness.

70   The nuns swept our hair back into high, bouffant hairstyles. This made us look more girlish and less inclined to eat people, the way that squirrels are saved from looking like rodents by their poofy tails. I was wearing a white organdy dress with orange polka dots. Jeanette was wearing a mauve organdy dress with blue polka dots. Linette was wearing a red organdy dress with white polka dots. Mirabella was in a dark corner, wearing a muzzle. Her party culottes were duct-taped to her knees. The nuns had tied little bows on the muzzle to make it more festive. Even so, the jazz band from West Toowoomba kept glancing nervously her way.

71   "You smell astoooounding!" Kyle was saying, accidentally stretching the diphthong into a howl and then blushing. "I mean—"

72   "Yes, I know what it is that you mean," I snapped. (That's probably a little narrative embellishment on my part; it must have been months before I could really "snap" out words.) I didn't smell astounding. I had rubbed a pumpkin muffin all over my body earlier that morning to mask my natural, feral scent. Now I smelled like a purebred girl, easy to kill. I narrowed my eyes at Kyle and flattened my ears, something I hadn't done for months. Kyle looked panicked,

trying to remember the words that would make me act like a girl again. I felt hot, oily tears squeezing out of the red corners of my eyes. Shoesonfeet! I barked at myself. I tried again. "My! What lovely weather—"

73   The jazz band struck up a tune.

74   "The time has come to do the Sausalito," Sister Maria announced, beaming into the microphone. "Every sister grab a brother!" She switched on Walter's industrial flashlight, struggling beneath its weight, and aimed the beam in the center of the room.

75   Uh-oh. I tried to skulk off into Mirabella's corner, but Kyle pushed me into the spotlight. "No," I moaned through my teeth, "noooooo." All of a sudden the only thing my body could remember how to do was pump and pump. In a flash of white-hot light, my months at St. Lucy's had vanished, and I was just a terrified animal again. As if of their own accord, my feet started to wiggle out of my shoes. Mouth shut, I gasped, staring down at my naked toes, mouthshutmouthshut.

76   "Ahem. The time has come," Sister Maria coughed, "to do the Sausalito." She paused. "The Sausalito," she added helpfully, "does not in any way resemble the thing that you are doing."

77   Beads of sweat stood out on my forehead. I could feel my jaws gaping open, my tongue lolling out of the left side of my mouth. What were the steps? I looked frantically for Jeanette; she would help me, she would tell me what to do.

78   Jeanette was sitting in the corner, sipping punch through a long straw and watching me pant. I locked eyes with her, pleading with the mute intensity that I had used to beg her for weasel bones in the forest. "What are the steps?" I mouthed.

79   "The steps!"

80   "The steps?" Then Jeanette gave me a wide, true wolf smile. For an instant, she looked just like our mother. "Not for you," she mouthed back.

81   I threw my head back, a howl clawing its way up my throat. I was about to lose all my Skill Points, I was about to fail my Adaptive Dancing test. But before the air could burst from my lungs, the wind got knocked out of me. Oomph! I fell to the ground, my skirt falling softly over my head. Mirabella had intercepted my eye-cry for help. She'd chewed through her restraints and tackled me from behind, barking at unseen cougars, trying to shield me with her tiny body. "Caramba!" Sister Maria squealed, dropping the flashlight. The music ground to a halt. And I have never loved someone so much, before or since, as I loved my littlest sister at that moment. I wanted to roll over and lick her ears, I wanted to kill a dozen spotted fawns and let her eat first.

Please note that excerpts and passages in the StudySync® library and this workbook are intended as touchstones to generate interest in an author's work. The excerpts and passages do not substitute for the reading of entire texts, and StudySync® strongly recommends that students seek out and purchase the whole literary or informational work in order to experience it as the author intended. Links to online resellers are available in our digital library. In addition, complete works may be ordered through an authorized reseller by filling out and returning to StudySync® the order form enclosed in this workbook.

Reading & Writing Companion   51

82   But everybody was watching; everybody was waiting to see what I would do. "I wasn't talking to you," I grunted from underneath her. "I didn't want your help. Now you have ruined the Sausalito! You have ruined the ball!" I said more loudly, hoping the nuns would hear how much my enunciation had improved.

83   "You have ruined it!" my sisters panted, circling around us, eager to close ranks. "Mirabella has ruined it!" Every girl was wild-eyed and itching under her polka dots, punch froth dribbling down her chin. The pack had been waiting for this moment for some time. "Mirabella cannot adapt! Back to the woods, back to the woods!"

84   The band from West Toowoomba had quietly packed their instruments into black suitcases and were sneaking out the back. The boys had fled back towards the lake, bow ties spinning, snapping suspenders in their haste. Mirabella was still snarling in the center of it all, trying to figure out where the danger was so that she could defend me against it. The nuns exchanged glances.

85   In the morning, Mirabella was gone. We checked under all the beds. I pretended to be surprised. I'd known she would have to be expelled the minute I felt her weight on my back. Walter came and told me this in secret after the ball, "So you can say yer good-byes." I didn't want to face Mirabella. Instead, I packed a tin lunch pail for her: two jelly sandwiches on saltine crackers, a chloroformed squirrel, a gilt-edged placard of St. Bolio. I left it for her with Sister Ignatius, with a little note: "Best wishes!" I told myself I'd done everything I could.

86   "Hooray!" the pack crowed. "Something has been done!"

87   We raced outside into the bright sunlight, knowing full well that our sister had been turned loose, that we'd never find her. A low roar rippled through us and surged up and up, disappearing into the trees. I listened for an answering howl from Mirabella, heart thumping—what if she heard us and came back? But there was nothing.

88   We graduated from St. Lucy's shortly thereafter. As far as I can recollect, that was our last communal howl.

. . .

89   Stage 5: At this point your students are able to interact effectively in the new cultural environment. They find it easy to move between the two cultures.

. . .

90   One Sunday, near the end of my time at St. Lucy's, the sisters gave me a special pass to go visit the parents. The woodsman had to accompany me; I

couldn't remember how to find the way back on my own. I wore my best dress and brought along some prosciutto and dill pickles in a picnic basket. We crunched through the fall leaves in silence, and every step made me sadder. "I'll wait out here," the woodsman said, leaning on a blue elm and lighting a cigarette.

91 The cave looked so much smaller than I remembered it. I had to duck my head to enter. Everybody was eating when I walked in. They all looked up from the bull moose at the same time, my aunts and uncles, my sloe-eyed, lolling cousins, the parents. My uncle dropped a thighbone from his mouth. My littlest brother, a cross-eyed wolf-boy who has since been successfully rehabilitated and is now a dour, balding children's book author, started whining in terror. My mother recoiled from me, as if I was a stranger. TRRR? She sniffed me for a long moment. Then she sank her teeth into my ankle, looking proud and sad. After all the tail wagging and perfunctory barking had died down, the parents sat back on their hind legs. They stared up at me expectantly, panting in the cool gray envelope of the cave, waiting for a display of what I had learned.

92 "So," I said, telling my first human lie. "I'm home."

"St. Lucy's Home for Girls Raised by Wolves" from ST. LUCY'S HOME FOR GIRLS RAISED BY WOLVES: STORIES by Karen Russell, copyright © 2006 by Karen Russell. Used by permission of Alfred A. Knopf, an imprint of the Knopf Doubleday Publishing Group, a division of Penguin Random House LLC. All rights reserved.

Please note that excerpts and passages in the StudySync® library and this workbook are intended as touchstones to generate interest in an author's work. The excerpts and passages do not substitute for the reading of entire texts, and StudySync® strongly recommends that students seek out and purchase the whole literary or informational work in order to experience it as the author intended. Links to online resellers are available in our digital library. In addition, complete works may be ordered through an authorized reseller by filling out and returning to StudySync® the order form enclosed in this workbook.

Reading & Writing Companion   53

ST. LUCY'S HOME FOR GIRLS
RAISED BY WOLVES

First Read

Read "St. Lucy's Home for Girls Raised by Wolves." After you read, complete the Think Questions below.

 THINK QUESTIONS

1. Why do the sisters treat Mirabella like an outcast? Cite specific evidence from the text to support your answer.

2. Why does Claudette repeat the mantra "shoes on feet" throughout the story? Cite specific evidence from the text to support your answer.

3. Why do the sisters believe they will never see Mirabella again? Cite specific evidence from the text to support your answer.

4. Use context clues to determine the meaning of the word **ostracized** as it is used in the story. Write your best definition of *ostracized* here and explain which clues helped you arrive at your answer.

5. The Latin prefix *con-* means "together" and the Latin root *-fer-* means "to bring or carry." Using this information and your knowledge of word patterns and relationships, write your best definition of the word **conferred** here.

Skill:
Compare and Contrast

Use the Checklist to analyze Compare and Contrast in "St. Lucy's Home for Girls Raised by Wolves."

••• CHECKLIST FOR COMPARE AND CONTRAST

In order to determine how to compare and contrast a text to its source material, use the following steps:

✓ first, choose works of literature in which the author draws on and transforms elements from another source

✓ next, identify literary elements that are comparable in the text and its source

- the series of events that make up each plot

- connections between the characters and what motivates them

- the theme in each work

- the message or ideas the authors want to communicate to readers

✓ finally, explain ways the author transforms the source material, perhaps by updating certain aspects of the plot or changing a character's traits

To analyze how an author draws on and transforms source material, consider the following questions:

✓ How does the author draw from the source material?

✓ How does the author transform the source material?

✓ How do the literary elements in the text compare to its source?

Please note that excerpts and passages in the StudySync® library and this workbook are intended as touchstones to generate interest in an author's work. The excerpts and passages do not substitute for the reading of entire texts, and StudySync® strongly recommends that students seek out and purchase the whole literary or informational work in order to experience it as the author intended. Links to online resellers are available in our digital library. In addition, complete works may be ordered through an authorized reseller by filling out and returning to StudySync® the order form enclosed in this workbook.

Reading & Writing Companion   **55**

Skill:
Compare and Contrast

Reread paragraph 35 of "St. Lucy's Home for Girls Raised by Wolves" and paragraphs 13 and 14 of *Braving the Wilderness*. Then, using the Checklist on the previous page, answer the multiple-choice questions below.

⟳ YOUR TURN

1. How are the consequences for not fitting in most similar for each girl?

   ○ A. Failure for both will mean being not being able to get a job.

   ○ B. Failure for both will mean rejection by their families.

   ○ C. Failure for both will mean not being part of a team.

   ○ D. Failure for both will mean getting expelled from school.

2. How are the consequences of not fitting in different for each girl?

   ○ A. Claudette won't belong anywhere ever again if she fails at school; Brown may one day find belonging elsewhere.

   ○ B. Claudette's parents will accept her failure gracefully; Brown's won't.

   ○ C. Brown's parents will accept her failure gracefully; Claudette's won't.

   ○ D. Claudette can join another pack if she fails at school; Brown can't join another family.

3. How are the themes in these passages similar?

   ○ A. Both suggest a theme about the importance of positive workplace relationships.

   ○ B. Both suggest a theme about the importance of respecting the wishes of one's elders.

   ○ C. Both suggest a theme about the negative impacts of failing to achieve membership in a group.

   ○ D. Both suggest a theme about the advantages of being in nature over being in a man-made environment.

Skill:
Allusion

Use the Checklist to analyze Allusion in "St. Lucy's Home for Girls Raised by Wolves." Refer to the sample student annotations about Allusion in the text.

••• CHECKLIST FOR ALLUSION

In order to identify an allusion, note the following:

✓ clues in a specific work that suggest a reference to previous source material

✓ the theme, event, character, or situation in a text to which the allusion adds information

To better understand the source material an author used to create a new work, do the following:

✓ use a print or digital resource to look up the work and any other allusions

✓ list details about the work or allusion that are related to the new work

To analyze how an author draws on and transforms source material in a specific work of fiction, consider the following questions:

✓ What theme/event/character from another work is referenced in the fiction I am reading? How do I know?

✓ How does that theme/event/character change or transform in "St. Lucy's Home for Girls Raised by Wolves"?

✓ What does the modern version of the story change or add to the earlier story?

Please note that excerpts and passages in the StudySync® library and this workbook are intended as touchstones to generate interest in an author's work. The excerpts and passages do not substitute for the reading of entire texts, and StudySync® strongly recommends that students seek out and purchase the whole literary or informational work in order to experience it as the author intended. Links to online resellers are available in our digital library. In addition, complete works may be ordered through an authorized reseller by filling out and returning to StudySync® the order form enclosed in this workbook.

Reading & Writing
Companion

57

Skill:
Allusion

Reread paragraphs 39–43 of "St. Lucy's Home for Girls Raised by Wolves." Then, using the Checklist on the previous page, answer the multiple-choice questions below.

↻ YOUR TURN

1. Which sentence contains an allusion to the source material, Ovid's *Metamorphoses*?

   ○ A. To correct a failing, you must first be aware of it as a failing.

   ○ B. Mirabella, battling a raccoon under the dinner table while the rest of us took dainty bites of peas and borscht.

   ○ C. I could have warned her.

   ○ D. She hated the spongy, long-dead foods we were served . . .

2. Which of the following statements alludes to the way Jupiter and the gods feel about Lycaon and the human race?

   ○ A. The nuns were worried about Mirabella, too.

   ○ B. "You have to pull your weight around here," we overheard Sister Josephine saying one night.

   ○ C. "Something must be done," Sister Ignatius said firmly. The other nuns nodded, a sea of thin, colorless lips and kettle-black brows.

   ○ D. That ominously passive construction; a something so awful that nobody wanted to assume responsibility for it.

3. Which of the following statements best describes a change in the way wolves are depicted in Karen Russell's "St. Lucy's Home for Girls Raised by Wolves" from the source material?

   ○ A. In Ovid's story, the transformation from human to wolf is the punishment, whereas in Russell's story, the transformation from wolf to human seems to be the punishment.

   ○ B. In Ovid's story, Lycaon was more civilized before he was transformed into a wolf, whereas the wolf-girls were never civilized.

   ○ C. Lycaon's transformation into a wolf was harder compared to the wolf-girls' transformation into civilized human girls.

   ○ D. In Russell's story, wolves are considered to be more acceptable in civilized society.

ST. LUCY'S HOME FOR GIRLS
RAISED BY WOLVES

Close Read

Reread "St. Lucy's Home for Girls Raised by Wolves." As you reread, complete the Skills Focus questions below. Then use your answers and annotations from the questions to help you complete the Write activity.

◎ SKILLS FOCUS

1. The short story "St. Lucy's Home for Girls Raised by Wolves" and the excerpt from the non-fiction text *Braving the Wilderness* both deal with the problem of fitting in. Identify evidence of how the desire to fit in causes conflict for Claudette. Then, in your annotation, explain how that conflict is similar to or different from the conflict faced by Brené Brown in *Braving the Wilderness*.

2. Identify a passage that reveals an important contrast between the setting of the woods and the setting of the school, and analyze how this contrast influences a theme about human society.

3. Identify a passage that reveals a conflict in Claudette's character and analyze how it shows her to be both complex and believable.

4. Identify a passage from the ball in which the setting causes conflict for a character, and explain how it influences a theme about the struggle to conform to new standards of behavior.

5. Identify an important moment in the plot near the end of the story, and explain how it helps develop a central theme about the consequences of trying to fit in.

✏ WRITE

LITERARY ANALYSIS: The short story "St. Lucy's Home for Girls Raised by Wolves" is a work of fiction and the excerpt from *Braving the Wilderness: The Quest for True Belonging and the Courage to Stand Alone* is a work of non-fiction. Both texts tell a story about the harsh consequences of not fitting into a community or group. Compare and contrast the ways in which the community in each story enhances the conflict faced by the main character and influences the theme.

Please note that excerpts and passages in the StudySync® library and this workbook are intended as touchstones to generate interest in an author's work. The excerpts and passages do not substitute for the reading of entire texts, and StudySync® strongly recommends that students seek out and purchase the whole literary or informational work in order to experience it as the author intended. Links to online resellers are available in our digital library. In addition, complete works may be ordered through an authorized reseller by filling out and returning to StudySync® the order form enclosed in this workbook.

Reading & Writing
Companion

59

Sure You Can Ask Me A Personal Question

POETRY
Diane Burns
1989

Introduction

Being an ambassador on behalf of a marginalized culture is an all-too-familiar situation for the speaker of "Sure You Can Ask Me a Personal Question." Through a series of responses to increasingly invasive questions, poet Diane Burns (1957–2006) depicts some of the difficult experiences that Native Americans and First Nations peoples must navigate in the modern world. Burns grew up on reservations in Wisconsin and North Dakota before moving to New York City and amassing a cult following for her work. *Riding the One-Eyed Ford*, her only poetry

"Oh, so you've had an Indian friend?"

NOTES

1   How do you do?

2   No, I am not Chinese.

3   No, not Spanish.

4   No, I am American Indi—uh, Native American.

5   No, not from India.

6   No, not Apache.

7   No, not Navajo.

8   No, not Sioux.

9   No, we are not **extinct**.

10 Yes, Indian.

11 Oh?

12 So that's where you got those high cheekbones.

13 Your great grandmother, huh?

14 An Indian Princess, huh?

15 Hair down to there?

16 Let me guess. Cherokee?

17 Oh, so you've had an Indian friend?

18 That close?

19 Oh, so you've had an Indian lover?

20 That tight?

21 Oh, so you've had an Indian servant?

22 That much?

23 Yeah, it was awful what you guys did to us.

24 It's real **decent** of you to **apologize**.

25 No, I don't know where you can get peyote[1].

26 No, I don't know where you can get Navajo rugs real cheap.

---

1. **peyote** a hallucinogenic drug derived from cacti.

Please note that excerpts and passages in the StudySync® library and this workbook are intended as touchstones to generate interest in an author's work. The excerpts and passages do not substitute for the reading of entire texts, and StudySync® strongly recommends that students seek out and purchase the whole literary or informational work in order to experience it as the author intended. Links to online resellers are available in our digital library. In addition, complete works may be ordered through an authorized reseller by filling out and returning to StudySync® the order form enclosed in this workbook.

Reading & Writing Companion   **61**

NOTES

27 No, I didn't make this. I bought it at Bloomingdales.

28 Thank you. I like your hair too.

29 I don't know if anyone knows whether or not Cher[2]

30 is really Indian.

31 No, I didn't make it rain tonight.

32 Yeah. Uh-huh. **Spirituality.**

33 Uh-huh. Yeah. Spirituality. Uh-huh. Mother

34 Earth. Yeah. Uh-huh. Uh-huh. Spirituality.

35 No, I didn't major in archery.

36 Yeah, a lot of us drink too much.

37 Some of us can't drink enough.

38 This ain't no **stoic** look.

39 This is my face.

From *Riding the One-Eyed Ford* by Diane Burns. Published 1981, Contact II/
Strawberry Press.

✏ WRITE

LITERARY ANALYSIS: Based on clues in the poem's language and structure, what attitude does the speaker have about the personal questions she is asked, and what message does the poet seek to convey to those who would presume to ask such questions?

---

2. **Cher** an American singer and actress

Angela's Ashes: A Memoir

INFORMATIONAL TEXT
Frank McCourt
1996

Introduction

Irish immigrant Frank McCourt (1930–2009) worked as a public school teacher in New York for 25 years before writing *Angela's Ashes: A Memoir*. His beloved recollection of his "miserable Irish childhood"—which won him a Pulitzer Prize in 1997—transports readers back to 1930s and '40s Ireland through harrowing stories of his poverty-stricken upbringing. The excerpt presented here focuses on young Frank's experience as a typhoid patient in a hospital in Limerick, where, during his stay, he befriends the girl in the neighboring room. Together, they fill their time by reading poetry and annoying their nurse, Sister Rita.

"There are twenty beds in the ward, all white, all empty."

NOTES

Skill:
Language,
Style, Audience

The language is informal. The phrase "yoo hoo, boy with the typhoid" gives the text a humorous, playful tone.

The author uses simple words and direct questions and answers that sound the way children speak.

from Chapter VIII

1 The room next to me is empty till one morning a girl's voice says, Yoo hoo, who's there?

2 I'm not sure if she's talking to me or someone in the room beyond.

3 Yoo hoo, boy with the typhoid[1], are you awake?

4 I am.

5 Are you better?

6 I am.

7 Well, why are you here?

8 I don't know. I'm still in the bed. They stick needles in me and give me medicine.

9 What do you look like?

10 I wonder, What kind of a question is that? I don't know what to tell her.

11 Yoo hoo, are you there, typhoid boy?

12 I am.

13 What's your name?

14 Frank.

15 That's a good name. My name is Patricia Madigan. How old are you?

16 Ten.

17 Oh. She sounds disappointed.

---

1. **typhoid** an infectious bacterial infection marked by a fever, intestinal inflammation, and ulceration

Reading & Writing Companion

18 But I'll be eleven in August, next month.

19 Well, that's better than ten. I'll be fourteen in September. Do you want to know why I'm in the Fever Hospital?

20 I do.

21 I have diphtheria[2] and something else.

22 What's something else?

23 They don't know. They think I have a disease from foreign parts because my father used to be in Africa. I nearly died. Are you going to tell me what you look like?

24 I have black hair.

25 You and millions.

26 I have brown eyes with bits of green that's called hazel.

27 You and thousands.

28 I have stitches on the back of my right hand and my two feet where they put in the soldier's blood.

29 Oh, God, did they?

30 They did.

31 You won't be able to stop marching and saluting.

32 There's a swish of habit and click of beads and then Sister Rita's voice. Now, now, what's this? There's to be no talking between two rooms especially when it's a boy and a girl. Do you hear me, Patricia?

33 I do, Sister.

34 Do you hear me, Francis?

35 I do, Sister.

36 You could be giving thanks for your two remarkable recoveries. You could be saying the rosary[3]. You could be reading *The Little Messenger of the Sacred Heart* that's beside your beds. Don't let me come back and find you talking.

37 She comes into my room and wags her finger at me. Especially you, Francis, after thousands of boys prayed for you at the Confraternity. Give thanks, Francis, give thanks.

---

2. **diphtheria** a disease affecting the throat, heart, and nervous system
3. **rosary** a set of prayers used by Roman Catholics

38   She leaves and there's silence for awhile. Then Patricia whispers, Give thanks, Francis, give thanks, and say your rosary, Francis, and I laugh so hard a nurse runs in to see if I'm all right. She's a very stern nurse from the County Kerry and she frightens me. What's this, Francis? Laughing? What is there to laugh about? Are you and that Madigan girl talking? I'll report you to Sister Rita. There's to be no laughing for you could be doing serious damage to your **internal apparatus**.

39   She plods out and Patricia whispers again in a heavy Kerry accent, No laughing, Francis, you could be doin' serious damage to your internal apparatus. Say your rosary, Francis, and pray for your internal apparatus.

. . .

40   Every day I can't wait for the doctors and nurses to leave me alone so I can learn a new verse from Patricia and find out what's happening to the highwayman and the landlord's red-lipped daughter. I love the poem because it's exciting and almost as good as my two lines of Shakespeare. The redcoats[4] are after the highwayman because they know he told her, I'll come to thee by moonlight, though hell should bar the way.

41   I'd love to do that myself, come by moonlight for Patricia in the next room, though hell should bar the way. She's ready to read the last few verses when in comes the nurse from Kerry shouting at her, shouting at me, I told ye there was to be no talking between rooms. Diphtheria is never allowed to talk to typhoid and visa versa. I warned ye. And she calls out, Seamus, take this one. Take the by. Sister Rita said one more word out of him and upstairs with him. We gave ye a warning to stop the blathering but ye wouldn't. Take the by, Seamus, take him.

42   Ah, now nurse, sure isn't he harmless. 'Tis only a bit o' poetry.

43   Take that by, Seamus, take him at once.

44   He bends over me and whispers, Ah, God, I'm sorry, Frankie. Here's your English history book. He slips the book under my shirt and lifts me from the bed. He whispers that I'm a feather. I try to see Patricia when we pass through her room but all I can make out is a blur of dark head on a pillow.

45   Sister Rita stops us in the hall to tell me I'm a great disappointment to her, that she expected me to be a good boy after what God had done for me, after all the prayers said by hundreds of boys at the Confraternity, after all the care from the nuns and nurses of the Fever Hospital, after the way they let my mother and father in to see me, a thing rarely allowed, and this is how I repaid them lying in the bed reciting silly poetry back and forth with Patricia Madigan

Skill:
Language,
Style, Audience

The unconventional word choice of "sure isn't he harmless" makes the dialogue sound old-fashioned.

The word "by" instead of "boy" is an example of Irish dialect. The tone is informal, but the style is commanding and adult.

---

4. **redcoats** soldiers in the British army

knowing very well there was a ban on all talk between typhoid and diphtheria. She says I'll have plenty of time to reflect on my sins in the big ward upstairs and I should beg God's forgiveness for my disobedience reciting a **pagan** English poem about a thief on a horse and a maiden with red lips who commits a terrible sin when I could have been praying or reading the life of a saint. She made it her business to read that poem so she did and I'd be well advised to tell the priest in **confession**.

46 The Kerry nurse follows us upstairs gasping and holding on to the banister. She tells me I better not get the notion she'll be running up to this part of the world every time I have a little pain or a twinge.

47 There are twenty beds in the ward, all white, all empty. The nurse tells Seamus put me at the far end of the ward against the wall to make sure I don't talk to anyone who might be passing the door, which is very unlikely since there isn't another soul on this whole floor. She tells Seamus this was the fever ward during the Great Famine[5] long ago and only God knows how many died here brought in too late for anything but a wash before they were buried and there are stories of cries and moans in the far reaches of the night. She says 'twould break your heart to think of what the English did to us, that if they didn't put the **blight** on the potato they didn't do much to take it off. No pity. No feeling at all for the people that died in this very ward, children suffering and dying here while the English feasted on roast beef and guzzled the best of wine in their big houses, little children with their mouths all green from trying to eat the grass in the fields beyond, God bless us and save us and guard us from future famines.

48 Seamus says 'twas a terrible thing indeed and he wouldn't want to be walking these halls in the dark with all the little green mouths gaping at him. The nurse takes my temperature, 'Tis up a bit, have a good sleep for yourself now that you're away from the chatter with Patricia Madigan below who will never know a gray hair.

49 She shakes her head at Seamus and he gives her a sad shake back.

50 Nurses and nuns never think you know what they're talking about. If you're ten going on eleven you're supposed to be simple like my uncle Pat Sheehan who was dropped on his head. You can't ask questions. You can't show you understand what the nurse said about Patricia Madigan, that she's going to die, and you can't show you want to cry over this girl who taught you a lovely poem which the nun says is bad.

Excerpted from *Angela's Ashes: A Memoir* by Frank McCourt, published by Simon & Schuster.

5. **Great Famine** a time of mass starvation and disease in Ireland from 1845 to 1849

First Read

Read *Angela's Ashes: A Memoir*. After you read, complete the Think Questions below.

1. Refer to details from the text that reveal how Sister Rita feels about fraternizing in the infirmary.

2. Write two or three sentences exploring the relationship between the Irish and English, as depicted in paragraph 47 of the text. Support your answer with direct quotations, as well as your own inferences.

3. What is bittersweet about Frank's friendship with Patricia? Refer to paragraph 50 in your response.

4. The Latin word *confiteri* means "to admit" or "to acknowledge." Using this information and your knowledge of word patterns and relationships, write your best definition of the word **confession** here.

5. Use context to determine the meaning of the word **blight** as it is used in the text. Write your definition of *blight* here and tell how you determined its meaning. Finally, consult a dictionary to verify your definition.

Skill:
Language, Style, and Audience

Use the Checklist to analyze Language, Style, and Audience in *Angela's Ashes: A Memoir*. Refer to the sample student annotations about Language, Style, and Audience in the text.

In order to determine an author's style, do the following:

- ✓ identify and define any unfamiliar words or phrases

- ✓ analyze the surrounding words and phrases as well as the context in which the specific words are being used

- ✓ note the audience—both intended and unintended—and possible reactions to the author's word choice and style

- ✓ examine your reaction to the author's word choice and how the author's choice affected your reaction

To analyze the cumulative impact of word choice on meaning and tone, ask the following questions:

- ✓ How did your understanding of the writer's language change during your analysis?

- ✓ How does the writer's cumulative word choice impact or create meaning in the text?

- ✓ How does the writer's cumulative word choice impact or create a specific tone in the text?

- ✓ What images, feelings, or ideas does the writer's cumulative word choice evoke?

- ✓ How could various audiences interpret this language? What different possible emotional responses can you list?

Please note that excerpts and passages in the StudySync® library and this workbook are intended as touchstones to generate interest in an author's work. The excerpts and passages do not substitute for the reading of entire texts, and StudySync® strongly recommends that students seek out and purchase the whole literary or informational work in order to experience it as the author intended. Links to online resellers are available in our digital library. In addition, complete works may be ordered through an authorized reseller by filling out and returning to StudySync® the order form enclosed in this workbook.

Reading & Writing
Companion

69

Skill:
Language, Style, and Audience

Reread paragraphs 48–50 of *Angela's Ashes: A Memoir*. Then, using the Checklist on the previous page, answer the multiple-choice questions below.

↻ YOUR TURN

1. How does the author's word choice in paragraph 48 contribute to the style and tone of the text?

   ○ A. The phrase "'twas a terrible thing indeed" contributes to the formal tone and style of the text.

   ○ B. The phrases "all the little green mouths gaping at him" and "away from the chatter of Patricia Madigan who will never know a gray hair" contribute to the colloquial, conversational style and an informal, though bleak, tone.

   ○ C. The use of complex, technical, and abstract language contributes to the academic style and formal tone of the text.

   ○ D. The long, complex sentences and lack of quotation marks give the text a strange, confusing voice and tone.

2. How does the author's specific word choice in paragraph 50 contribute to the style and tone of the text?

   ○ A. The many short, simple sentences give the text an informal style, and the language conveys a cheerful tone.

   ○ B. The use of many compound-complex sentences give the text a formal style, and the language conveys a celebratory tone.

   ○ C. The repetition of the word "you" gives the text an informal, conversational style, and the language conveys a disapproving tone.

   ○ D. The nontraditional word choice in the first sentence gives the text a nontraditional style, and language conveys a supportive tone.

Close Read

Angela's Ashes: A Memoir. As you reread, complete the Skills Focus questions below. Then use your answers and annotations from the questions to help you complete the Write activity.

◎ SKILLS FOCUS

1. Identify a passage in which the author of *Angela's Ashes: A Memoir* uses specific word choice and style to help the reader distinguish and describe Patricia's voice. Explain how the author's stylistic choices contribute to developing Patricia's voice.

2. Identify specific word choice in paragraphs 37 and 38 that establishes a tone of hopefulness and humor. Explain how the author's word choice and stylistic choices contribute to this tone.

3. Highlight details in the story that reveal what Patricia and the poem represent to Frank. Use original commentary to explain what the details reveal explicitly and implicitly.

4. In both "Sure You Can Ask Me a Personal Question" and the excerpt from *Angela's Ashes: A Memoir*, individuals' identities are defined by others in simplistic, often stereotypical terms. Identify a passage in *Angela's Ashes: A Memoir* when this happens to the narrator, and annotate to compare it to a similar experience of the speaker in the poem.

5. Identify details in paragraph 50 that reveal the author's explicit message about what some adults think about children. Then, identify an implicit message that is conveyed through this explicit message. Explain your interpretation.

✏ WRITE

LITERARY ANALYSIS: Although it consists mainly of dialogue, this memoir excerpt contains no quotation marks. How does the author's use of language and style enable readers to distinguish between the voices of the characters, give those characters personality, and establish a tone? Use original commentary to support your response.

Please note that excerpts and passages in the StudySync® library and this workbook are intended as touchstones to generate interest in an author's work. The excerpts and passages do not substitute for the reading of entire texts, and StudySync® strongly recommends that students seek out and purchase the whole literary or informational work in order to experience it as the author intended. Links to online resellers are available in our digital library. In addition, complete works may be ordered through an authorized reseller by filling out and returning to StudySync® the order form enclosed in this workbook.

Reading & Writing Companion

71

Why I Lied to Everyone in High School About Knowing Karate

INFORMATIONAL TEXT
Jabeen Akhtar
2017

Introduction

Jabeen Akhtar is a Pakistani American author who was raised in Washington, D.C. and spent ten years working for the federal government before turning to writing. In this essay, she remembers an instance in the tenth grade when the staff of her high school yearbook wanted to take a photo of her demonstrating her karate skills. The only problem? Jabeen had lied about knowing karate, wanting to stand out in some way, and throughout the experience she grapples with whether or not to tell the truth. The essay offers a glimpse into the pressures of high achievement that the children of immigrants often face from their parents—especially those kids who do not naturally excel at academics—and how difficult it can be to

"A lie could help fill the bland, infinite void of mediocrity."

NOTES

1 In 10th grade, I was chosen to be photographed for a yearbook feature called "Out of the Ordinary Hobbies." The yearbook staff heard I had a green belt in karate and wanted to do an interview with photos. Anna, a yearbook editor, approached me about the feature while I was organizing my locker.

2 "How did you know I knew karate?" I asked her.

3 She said Rodney told her, who heard it from Julie. Or maybe Heather. I didn't remember telling Julie. Or Heather.

Author yearbook photo, 1990

4 "I mean, a green belt, wow," Anna said. "Not many people have those types of skills." Anna said she always wanted to take a self-defense class. Why didn't the school offer karate instead of stupid stuff like home economics? She'd rather know how to protect herself than sew a button. Maybe I could give her a few pointers, she said, show her what to do if someone attacks her with a knife from behind.

5 I nodded along as Anna spoke, pulling textbooks from my backpack and stacking them in my locker where the poetry collection I had written for third period English sat visibly on the bottom shelf. "SMERSH" the title of the collection said, which was also the name of Stalin's counterintelligence agency. Below it was the subheading, "Death to Spies." It was 1990, and though the Cold War[1] had recently smashed into pieces, wall by wall, mallet by mallet, we still spoke its language. It was no surprise to me that things like the USSR, KGB, dead drops, poisoned lipsticks and *perestroika* would find their way into the stanzas of my electric typewriter-printed pages. Besides, poetry, I had decided, need not be tedious ruminations on flowers or **pallid** reflections on grief.

6 My English teacher had disagreed. "Too James Bond," she wrote across the title page, marking it with a "C." I placed my civics book over the top of it, hoping Anna didn't see my grade.

---

1. **Cold War** a period of political and economic tension between the United States and the Soviet Union

7   "The yearbook feature is new so we really want the best of the best," Anna said. "So tell me . . . are you in?"

8   Mary Lynn entered the hallway, her wall of freshly lacquered bangs holding steadfast as she shuffled past us towards her boyfriend's locker. She was one of the few headbangers to penetrate the wealthy student government crowd, however **tenuously**. She glanced at me over her Trapper Keeper, her eyes a mix of curiosity and mild indignation. No one ever stopped by my locker to talk to me and now here was someone from the yearbook staff and the visit looked official. Clearly, I had been chosen, out of the entire student body, for something in the yearbook. Something important. Which meant that in some capacity, I was important.

9   I couldn't blame for Mary Lynn for being skeptical.

10   Anna's pencil anxiously tapped her notebook. She was waiting for a response. I stuck my hand deep within the bowels of my locker, searching for a purple scrunchie and in my mind, searching for a way to tell her.

11   "Well?" she asked again. "Will you do the yearbook feature? Are you in?"

12   I'd been here before, in this same position years ago, and I knew what I needed to do. I needed to stop what I had set in motion. Stop things before they went any further, before they perilously and **irrevocably** went too far. I needed to tell Anna the truth.

13   I'd never had a day of karate in my life.

14   I looked down again at my locker, where my "C" hid under a pile of textbooks. I zipped up my backpack and swung the locker door shut.

15   "I'm in," I told her.

· · ·

16   Later that night, I picked through my closet selecting an outfit for the feature. I wanted to look stylish, but not trying-too-hard. Acid washed jeans rolled at the ankle. A black top with green stitching at the collar, silver hoop earrings. Black pleather Oxfords from Payless.

17   What other hobbies would be featured in the yearbook, I wondered? Things like sculpting, knitting, skydiving? That short guy David with the Eddie Van Halen waves and sleeveless jean jackets was always working on fancy cars at his father's auto shop — VW Bugs, Camaros, convertible Beemers and Saabs. I wonder if he'd be in it. Maybe he'd see my profile next to his and seek me out after school. "Hey, man, I saw that you do karate. Sweet!" he'd say. Maybe he'd give me a lift home in one of his cars, tell me all about the new catalytic converter he's installing in a Porsche 911 Carrera.

18 I put a New Order tape in the cassette player and turned up the volume:

19 *I feel so extraordinary.*

20 *Something's got a hold on me . . .*

21 I bounced around a little as I hung a rejected cream sweater and two pairs of pants back in the closet. In the privacy of my room, I allowed myself to feel it: the energy, my rapid heart rate, a growing sense of excitement.

22 I was going to be in a yearbook feature!

23 *I used to think that the day would never come . . .*

Yearbook feature, 1990

24 The list of reasons why this would never happen for me was extensive. I was an average student — C's mostly, sometimes skating by with a B minus. I would never make the cut for "Most Likely to Succeed." I was too short, my hands were bony, my lips were too big, and my eyebrows were too thick, so no chance for "Best Looking." Boys weren't interested in me, so "Best Looking Couple" or "Best Dressed Couple" or any iteration of "couple" was out. I told myself it was just the popular kids voting for each other in those categories anyway. It would carry on decades later in the corporate world over promotions and million-dollar hedge funds.

25 But I always wanted to be a superlative, to have a special place in those black and white pages or in the consciousness of my peers. I knew it would never happen based on merit, based on who I really was. So I told a lie. A lie was a shortcut to grandeur. A lie could help fill the bland, infinite void of mediocrity.

26 The truth would not lead me to recognition or honors, a lesson I had learned early on. When I was in 5th grade, I wrote a short story for my English class called "The Dinner Guest." It was about a man at a dinner party telling the woman seated next to him a thrilling story about a murderer whose right leg was shorter than the left. After the man finishes his story and gets up from the table, the woman gasps as she notices one of his legs is shorter than the other.

27 The story was dark and complex, but much to my surprise, everyone loved it. My English teacher passed it around the school, and the next day, I was informed it was the best story of the year. I was named the winner of the 1985 Wolftrap Elementary Author's Award, and, as all winners did, I was to read my story to the entire school at the next assembly.

28   It should have been a hallmark of achievement for a 10-year-old girl who was a middling student, barely visible to her teachers, one who still fumbled trying to braid her own hair.

29   But it wasn't a hallmark, or any sort of moment to look back on with pride. All week I had tried and failed, over and over, to write a story of my own, growing increasingly desperate as the clock ticked on. The night before the story was due, I plucked an anthology off my older sister's nightstand and leafed through it until I found a story I liked. It was called "The Dinner Guest." I didn't simply lift the plot or copy a few sentences. Besieged by an **odious** combination of panic and laziness, I copied the entire story word for word, even the title. And now I was going to have to read it at the assembly, in front of everyone, where surely someone in my school would recognize the story and I'd get caught for plagiarism.

30   What would my father say? He was already unhappy with my struggles in school, unhappy with how I was turning out. He'd leave newspaper clippings of child prodigies on my desk in my room. The last one had been about an Indian boy in California who was able to do calculus at age 4, graduated college at 12 and was on his way to becoming the world's youngest doctor at 17. Maybe my father thought it would serve as inspiration. *Look at this boy. Look how exceptional he is. You can be like him.*

31   Maybe my father thought **exceptionality** wasn't asking too much of me. We belonged to a coveted brand of immigrants — educated, hard-working and productive. The type of immigrants America loves. The type who come here from what white people often understand to be primitive third-world jungles and become doctors at 17. The standard-bearers of the bootstrap-pulling-to-riches ideal of the American Dream[2]. Immigrants like us are purposeful. We are let in on the condition that we will promote a fanciful, egalitarian narrative of America. And as long as we continually strive, achieve and contribute, go above and beyond, showcase extraordinary talent, and become exceptional citizens, we can stay.

32   To earn our keep in America, in other words, we must be like that boy.

33   But what if we're not like that boy?

34   What if we're like me?

35   A few nights before I had plagiarized the short story, my father sat with me at the kitchen table, going over the geometry test my teacher had sent directly to my parents with a note. I was averaging a "D" in class and hadn't done well on the test, now marked up by my teacher in red ink. I never knew what the note said.

36   "This is a 90 degree angle," my father told me, his finger tapping on the image he had drawn in my spiral notebook. "Now let's widen it." Using a

---

2. **American Dream** the national ideal that everyone in the United States can be successful if he or she works hard enough

compass, he drew another half-circle with lines through it and asked what type of angle it was.

37 I looked at the compass — the etching in the metal, the pointed spears — and traced my finger along the new design. I said it was a right angle.

38 "No," my father answered. "Acute."

39 He reached across the table for the protractor he had recently purchased for me. The other kids in class had clear plastic protractors. Mine was electric blue.

40 "Now we'll draw an angle here," he said. "What is this one? It's called . . . what?"

41 The blue color was a ploy. It didn't make this fun, or less intimidating. I looked at the compass, then back at my test, then back at the drawing.

42 "We went over this, remember?" my father said, his voice rising. "What angle did I just draw?"

43 It was getting late. My siblings had gone to bed.

44 "A right angle," I said.

45 "This is not a right angle."

46 He flipped through my spiral notebook and drew a giant "X" on a blank page. He went over everything again, drawing and drawing and drawing. Parallel lines, perpendicular lines, right angles, acute angles, obtuse angles, straight angles. He drew a little box where two lines intersected, asking what type of angle it was. "This is an easy one," he said.

47 I felt myself shrinking in my seat. I looked at the phone attached to the wall, the yellow cord spiraling down, the plastic jug of cherry Kool-Aid on the counter, anywhere I could for answers. "I . . . I don't know . . ."

48 Almost immediately, my father's glasses were off his head, torn from his face. He threw them onto the table. The sound of gold-plated chrome and glass crashing then skittering across wood echoed through the kitchen and into the dark living room, startling me. I let out a tiny, hurried shriek.

49 Then the world went black. My father's arms were around me, encasing me, the scent of drug store cologne overwhelming the air as I started to cry. Tears fell onto the bottom of his white dress shirt and pooled into one, damp spot.

50 My father pulled me in closer. Did he ever tell me about the time he was visited by a Jinn[3], he asked me? His voice sounded jubilant now, his frustration with me gone. I grabbed a fistful of his shirt to hold onto.

___

3. **Jinn** (Arabic) genie

51 He was just a little boy, my father said, my age, maybe 10 or 11, washing mungra beans in the garden of his mother's home in Kasur for the evening's supper, when a Jinn appeared before him. The Jinn told my father his arms were magical. They could wrap themselves around anything and form an impenetrable barrier. "My skinny arms," my father asked the Jinn? "Yes," said the Jinn. "Don't let size fool you." Those arms were like steel. Nothing could get through. Anything within those arms would be safe, the Jinn told him, protected from all the evils of the world.

52 If he could, my father said, he would keep me in his magical arms forever. Keep me protected. But he couldn't. He had to let me go, unravel his arms and let me out. So he just wanted me to do better. That's all. Do a little better so that when I'd be out there in the world, I'd be so great, so powerful that no one would ever dare mess with me. People like us in this country, we are always foreigners, no matter what our papers say, and they can take away who we are or what we have at any point. That is a fear he lives with every day, my father said. A fear he has for his children. We have to do great things, be important people, be really amazing, so that they like us, and want to keep us, and not do those bad things to us. Did I understand, my father asked? Did I understand what he was saying?

53 I understood. And I would for the rest of my life. This wasn't just about not doing well in school. This wasn't just about disappointing my father. My average grades, my average intellect, my average skills, my utter, **intractable** averageness, was a risk to my very being. I understood that I was just one more C, one more report card barren of celebratory gold and silver stickers, from being a forfeiture on the America-immigrant contract.

· · ·

54 A few days after my short story was passed around the school, I got a note from the principal. "Please see me in my office."

55 This was it. I was caught.

56 I clutched the note in my hand, damp from perspiration, as I walked past a 1st-grader banging on a xylophone, and a darkened room with kindergartners asleep on gym mats, to the center of the school where the administrators worked. I found the principal behind a Formica desk, straightening her nude pantyhose.

57 "Have a seat," she said.

58 I dutifully sat on an oversize plastic chair, my feet dangling over the metal legs.

59 "I want to assure you that I, personally, loved your story," the principal said. But it was too violent for the kindergartners, she explained, so she'd rather me not

read it during the assembly. Instead, would I be okay with this dot-matrix certificate and a few Strawberry Shortcake pencils?

60   I told her I was fine with her decision, even agreed my story would not be appropriate for a younger audience, looking like the most mature and gracious fifth grader she had ever seen. I left her office with my new pencils and once home, showed the certificate to my parents. "We are so proud of you," my father said. My parents were going to frame it, show their Pakistani friends how talented a writer their daughter was. Which wall to hang it on, they wondered? They argued over the best spot. I could hear them as I went upstairs, back into my sister's room. I found the anthology still on her nightstand, ripped the story out, and kept ripping until "The Dinner Guest" had disintegrated in my hands.

• • •

61   The Author's Award for my plagiarized story would remain my singular achievement for the next five years. By the time I reached high school, not much had changed. I still struggled academically. I still tried to be exceptional. But the pursuit of exceptionality is consuming, never-ending. If you can't be exceptional in one area of your life, you'd have to strive for it in another, then another, then another.

62   I decided I wasn't going to be exceptional academically, so maybe I could be socially. That seemed the next logical step.

63   In 10th grade, I was the periphery girl in my group of friends, the hanger-on, my status always in question. I wasn't the first person Christy bragged to if a boy got flirty in P.E. class, and Shannon didn't offer me rides home after school. My inclusion in group activities was hit or miss. I once saw Christy and the other girls in the group, Shannon and Michelle, meeting at the locker of another girl, Rebecca, before a pep rally so they could enter the gym together, something that had to have been coordinated in advance. Whatever note had been drawn up in class with instructions and maybe a heart or rainbow sketch was never passed to my desk. I entered the gym alone. I sat on the bleachers near the exit with a few teachers as cheerleaders kicked up their legs in red and black uniforms, the cheers and howls and stomping emanating from a crowd intoxicated on school spirit.

64   On Mondays, I'd hear about my friends' misadventures at the mall. Eric and his hot rich friend who went to that all-boys private school in Maryland were skateboarding in the parking lot when they ran into Christy and Michelle. After hitting up the food court for some Asian Express, the four of them went to Tower Records where Eric tried to steal a Smiths cassette and got caught. The manager kicked them out and Christy was still worried her mother would find out.

65   In class, I'd hear other groups of girls giggling and whispering about their own mall dramas from the weekend, something that always baffled me. Every time I went to the mall, no one was ever there except parents with little kids and the occasional sketchy mustached man in the indoor playground area. It was like every girl in high school knew which nights to congregate at the mall except me. Like there was some popular fun girl signal put out over the city but instead of a bat it was a silhouette of Patrick Swayze and my curtains were always drawn.

66   But maybe, with everyone thinking I knew karate, maybe with the yearbook feature, all of that could change.

67   Maybe, in the yearbook, the name "Jabeen Akhtar" would appear in large letters, larger than any of my friends'. It would force them to do a double-take, to look at me anew, with fresh eyes.

68   *She knows karate?* they'd ask.

69   *Yes, I do*, I would answer. *I know karate. Bet you didn't know that, did you?*

70   Maybe the yearbook feature would prove that I deserved a little air time, some recognition. Something more than just the little square photo with the masses. The yearbook feature could say what I couldn't to my friends and peers and teachers over the span of ten years roaming the school hallways alone: *look at me.*

. . .

71   The day arrived that Anna had scheduled for the feature. I met her and a photographer behind the school after 6th period. Anna asked for a quote about karate, and I told her about the importance of concentration and timing. Then the photographer told me to stand in front of the red brick wall **adjacent** to the cafeteria.

72   "Ok, Jabeen," he said, readying his camera. "This is it. Show us what you got. Go!"

73   My fists clenched. My leg shot up, and black Costco socks poked out of rolled-up acid-washed jeans.

74   "Wow!" Anna said. "What a kick!"

75   A few hours later, I sat at my desk in my room. I fidgeted in my chair, too small now to contain my puberty-widened hips. I thought about the feature, what it would look like when it came out in the yearbook, if I'd look pretty. If I'd feel ashamed seeing another one of my lies memorialized in print, just like the Author's Award still hanging on the wall on the floor beneath me.

76   I hadn't wanted things to go this far. I'd just wanted to be exceptional. To not be average. To allay my father's fears, to show him I could earn my keep like that boy in the article.

77   I tugged at the electric blue protractor, now scuffed and marked, faded with time. I remembered that day at the kitchen table.

78   But I wasn't like that boy. I wasn't exceptional. I wasn't a child prodigy, or a good student or a talented writer. I wasn't popular. And I didn't know karate. This was who I truly was, a composite of negatives, a person defined by all she is not.

79   That Jinn had been wrong about one thing. There was one thing my father's arms couldn't protect me from: myself.

80   I could fool everyone, but I knew the truth. I knew the real me. And all the lying and cheating and stupid things I did could no longer mask this unequivocal fact.

81   I pulled out some loose stationery from the top drawer and grabbed a pen.

82   "Dear Anna," I began to write. I asked her to please not publish the photo. The truth is, I explained to her, I'd never had a day of karate in my life. I must have told someone I knew karate for . . . I don't even know what reason, but I never thought it would get around the school this way. I was sorry for lying to her, sorry for wasting her time.

83   When I saw Anna the next day, she was heading to lunch with a small crowd. I held the note and steadied my breathing.

84   I could do this, I thought. I could do what I should have done the day Anna first approached me at my locker.

85   Maybe I was so busy lying and cheating that I never gave myself a fair chance. Maybe if I stepped out of my own way, I really could be an exceptional person someday, do something to make my father proud. Do something to truly deserve a place in the yearbook as an "out of the ordinary" girl. I could start right here, at this very moment. I could start by telling her the truth.

86   Anna saw me and waved. "Hey, Jabeen!" she yelled.

87   The sound reverberated down the hall — the sound of my name, whizzing past classrooms and bulletin boards and French Club announcements and Walkmans and letter jackets and students with their heads buried in their lockers. Anna's friends looked up. Other people looked up.

88   And at me.

89 They looked at me.

90 I turned the note over in my hand.

91 "Hey," I yelled back.

92 I crumpled the note in my pocket, turned and walked to my next class.

93 Maybe I'd tell the truth next time.

*Names have been changed

By Jabeen Akhtar, 2018. First appeared in Longreads. Used by permission of Jabeen Akhtar.

✏ WRITE

EXPLANATORY ESSAY: Write an explanatory essay that uses textual evidence to answer the question posed by the title: Why did Jabeen Akhtar lie to everyone in high school about knowing karate? Support your response about Jabeen's motivations with key details provided throughout the text about her high-school status, previous experiences, pressures, desires, fears, and dilemmas.

Welcome to America

POETRY
Sara Abou Rashed
2016

Introduction

The poetry and prose of Sara Abou Rashed (b. 1999) often focuses on her experiences as a refugee of Syria. Palestinian by origin but born and raised in Syria, her family fled the raging civil war and relocated to Columbus, Ohio. She quickly learned English and became an award-winning performance poet. Rashed first performed her one-woman poetry and prose show, *A Map of Myself,* at the Columbus Lincoln Theater and the Columbus Museum of Art in 2018. A meditation on the themes of home, art and the immigrant experience, "Welcome to America" was published in *Pudding Magazine* and featured in the *Huffington Post*.

"...your American dream / is my dream, I am afraid of what you're afraid of."

1 *Bring us your oppressed, your exhausted bodies,*
2 *your hungry, unheard crowds and we shall set them free*

3 "I'd like to welcome you to the one and only,
4 the greatest America." Says the lady
5 in the white shirt behind a desk.

6 "Now honey, please fill out all these papers,
7 and don't forget to send us your story,
8 why you came here, your hopes and expectations.
9 We wish you a happy life."

        ...

10 16 springs I've witnessed, not one
11 was blooming, there,
12 behind the shores of the Mediterranean,
13 everything is a **martyr**, there –
14 we don't dare live **lest** we die,
15 even roses grow stripped of colors.

16 Though, the scarred walls there memorize
17 our names, though the tarred roads
18 there know our stories.

19 But here,
20 to every ally, to every town,
21 I must introduce myself:

22 No, no, I am sorry, I am not who
23 you think I am.
24 No, I am not who they say I am.

25 See,
26 I am as much of a human as you are;
27 I brush my teeth, I sleep, I cry when hurt and bleed when injured,
28 I walk the land you walk, I breathe
29 the same air you breathe, your American dream
30 is my dream, I am afraid of what you're afraid of.

31 Please, don't stop me on streets to ask what Jihad[1] is,
32 don't mistake me for one of them, don't stare at me like an alien,
33 like a one-eyed, four-legged, green monster of your nightmares.

34 I am a woman of faith,
35 a citizen not a suspect.
36 I carry a breaking heart within, I hold mics not guns —
37 my story refuses to be told in bullets and word limits.

38 And no, I don't celebrate the death of children,
39 I don't wish to destroy homes and churches.

40 Trust me, I know what loss smells like:
41 the way fear and revolution play tug of war
42 on doorsteps, uproot loved ones from
43 framed pictures on walls, steal a father
44 from the dinner table — I can only hope
45 mine hears me now.

46 I know what loss smells like from a mile far, the way friends
47 tell you they saw your house tear **asunder**
48 like it was never there:
49 the old gate, the dolls, grandma's garden and every
50 dream we've built on the roof with hands too small
51 to plant hatred.

52 Still, some fear me, they call me names, they try to break
53 me, to wreck me, to **ricochet** me, but
54 my spine will keep mountains standing,
55 my knees will only ever kneel to my Lord:

56 Lord, make us whole again, all of us, make us human again,
57 forgive us for we have sinned, and Lord,
58 guide them to see me for who I am,
59 because I, too yearn for peace, because I drop poems, not bombs.

By Sara Abou Rashed, 2016. Used by permission of Sara Abou Rashed.

✏ WRITE

DISCUSSION: To what extent can Rashed's poem "Welcome to America" be considered an argumentative piece? What might Rashed's claim be? What examples of imagery might support her claim? What emotional appeals might she provide to convey her message?

---

1. **Jihad** Arabic word denoting an internal spiritual struggle against sin or the enemies of Islam

I Have a Dream

ARGUMENTATIVE TEXT

Martin Luther King, Jr.
1963

Introduction

On August 28, 1963, civil rights leader Dr. Martin Luther King Jr. (1929–1968) stood on the steps of the Lincoln Memorial and delivered his iconic "I Have a Dream" speech to a crowd of more than 250,000 people. King was a leader of the civil rights movement in America at the time and was a masterful orator, invoking history and religious doctrine, employing the power of rhetoric, and courageously speaking truth to power. From the moment it was delivered, "I Have a Dream" has been revered as one of the most powerful speeches in American history. The following year, at the age of 35, King became the youngest person ever to

"Now is the time to make real the promises of democracy."

1   I am happy to join with you today in what will go down in history as the greatest demonstration for freedom in the history of our nation.

2   Five score years ago, a great American, in whose symbolic shadow we stand today, signed the Emancipation Proclamation[1]. This momentous decree came as a great beacon light of hope to millions of Negro slaves who had been seared in the flames of withering injustice. It came as a joyous daybreak to end the long night of their captivity.

3   But one hundred years later, the Negro still is not free. One hundred years later, the life of the Negro is still sadly crippled by the manacles of segregation and the chains of discrimination. One hundred years later, the Negro lives on a lonely island of poverty in the midst of a vast ocean of material **prosperity**. One hundred years later, the Negro is still languished in the corners of American society and finds himself an exile in his own land. And so we've come here today to dramatize a shameful condition.

4   In a sense we've come to our nation's capital to cash a check. When the architects of our republic wrote the magnificent words of the Constitution and the Declaration of Independence, they were signing a promissory note to which every American was to fall heir. This note was a promise that all men, yes, black men as well as white men, would be guaranteed the "unalienable Rights" of "Life, Liberty and the pursuit of Happiness." It is obvious today that America has defaulted on this promissory note, insofar as her citizens of color are concerned. Instead of honoring this sacred obligation, America has given the Negro people a bad check, a check which has come back marked "**insufficient** funds."

5   But we refuse to believe that the bank of justice is bankrupt. We refuse to believe that there are insufficient funds in the great vaults of opportunity of this nation. And so, we've come to cash this check, a check that will give us upon demand the riches of freedom and the security of justice.

6   We have also come to this hallowed spot to remind America of the fierce urgency of Now. This is no time to engage in the luxury of cooling off or to take the tranquilizing drug of gradualism. Now is the time to make real the

---

1. **Emancipation Proclamation** an executive order signed by President Abraham Lincoln in 1863 decreeing enslaved people in the Confederacy to be freed

 Skill:
Arguments
and Claims

King states his position on the topic near the beginning of the speech and tells the audience what he wants them to believe. He continues to mention time to prove his position.

NOTES

promises of democracy. Now is the time to rise from the dark and desolate valley of segregation to the sunlit path of racial justice. Now is the time to lift our nation from the quicksands of racial injustice to the solid rock of brotherhood. Now is the time to make justice a reality for all of God's children.

7 It would be fatal for the nation to overlook the urgency of the moment. This sweltering summer of the Negro's **legitimate** discontent will not pass until there is an invigorating autumn of freedom and equality. Nineteen sixty-three is not an end, but a beginning. And those who hope that the Negro needed to blow off steam and will now be content will have a rude awakening if the nation returns to business as usual. And there will be neither rest nor tranquility in America until the Negro is granted his citizenship rights. The whirlwinds of revolt will continue to shake the foundations of our nation until the bright day of justice emerges.

8 But there is something that I must say to my people, who stand on the warm threshold which leads into the palace of justice: In the process of gaining our rightful place, we must not be guilty of wrongful deeds. Let us not seek to satisfy our thirst for freedom by drinking from the cup of bitterness and hatred. We must forever conduct our struggle on the high plane of dignity and discipline. We must not allow our creative protest to degenerate into physical violence. Again and again, we must rise to the majestic heights of meeting physical force with soul force.

9 The marvelous new militancy which has engulfed the Negro community must not lead us to a distrust of all white people, for many of our white brothers, as evidenced by their presence here today, have come to realize that their destiny is tied up with our destiny. And they have come to realize that their freedom is **inextricably** bound to our freedom.

10 We cannot walk alone.

11 And as we walk, we must make the pledge that we shall always march ahead.

12 We cannot turn back.

Skill:
Rhetoric

King begins each sentence with the same phrase and ends each sentence in present tense about a current injustice. This technique strengthens his argument by focusing on their shared experiences and how they must never give up.

13 There are those who are asking the devotees of civil rights, "When will you be satisfied?" We can never be satisfied as long as the Negro is the victim of the unspeakable horrors of police brutality. We can never be satisfied as long as our bodies, heavy with the fatigue of travel, cannot gain lodging in the motels of the highways and the hotels of the cities. We cannot be satisfied as long as the negro's basic mobility is from a smaller ghetto to a larger one. We can never be satisfied as long as our children are stripped of their self-hood and robbed of their dignity by signs stating: "For Whites Only." We cannot be satisfied as long as a Negro in Mississippi cannot vote and a Negro in New York believes he has nothing for which to vote. No, no, we are not satisfied, and we will not be satisfied until "justice rolls down like waters, and righteousness like a mighty stream."

14 I am not unmindful that some of you have come here out of great trials and tribulations. Some of you have come fresh from narrow jail cells. And some of

you have come from areas where your quest for freedom left you battered by the storms of **persecution** and staggered by the winds of police brutality. You have been the veterans of creative suffering. Continue to work with the faith that unearned suffering is redemptive. Go back to Mississippi, go back to Alabama, go back to South Carolina, go back to Georgia, go back to Louisiana, go back to the slums and ghettos of our northern cities, knowing that somehow this situation can and will be changed.

15 Let us not wallow in the valley of despair, I say to you today, my friends.

16 And so even though we face the difficulties of today and tomorrow, I still have a dream. It is a dream deeply rooted in the American dream.

17 I have a dream that one day this nation will rise up and live out the true meaning of its creed: "We hold these truths to be self-evident, that all men are created equal."

18 I have a dream that one day on the red hills of Georgia, the sons of former slaves and the sons of former slave owners will be able to sit down together at the table of brotherhood.

19 I have a dream that one day even the state of Mississippi, a state sweltering with the heat of injustice, sweltering with the heat of oppression, will be transformed into an oasis of freedom and justice.

20 I have a dream that my four little children will one day live in a nation where they will not be judged by the color of their skin but by the content of their character.

21 I have a *dream* today!

22 I have a dream that one day, down in Alabama, with its vicious racists, with its governor having his lips dripping with the words of "interposition" and "nullification" — one day right there in Alabama little black boys and black girls will be able to join hands with little white boys and white girls as sisters and brothers.

23 I have a *dream* today!

24 I have a dream that one day every valley shall be exalted, and every hill and mountain shall be made low, the rough places will be made plain, and the crooked places will be made straight; "and the glory of the Lord shall be revealed and all flesh shall see it together."

25 This is our hope, and this is the faith that I go back to the South with.

26 With this faith, we will be able to hew out of the mountain of despair a stone of hope. With this faith, we will be able to transform the jangling discords of our nation into a beautiful symphony of brotherhood. With this faith, we will be able

Skill:
Rhetoric

King speaks of two opposing ideas to create contrasting images in the audience's minds, which appeals to their emotions by drawing attention to the difference between their hopes for the future and the reality they currently experience.

to work together, to pray together, to struggle together, to go to jail together, to stand up for freedom together, knowing that we will be free one day.

27 And this will be the day — this will be the day when all of God's children will be able to sing with new meaning:

28 *My country 'tis of thee, sweet land of liberty, of thee I sing. Land where my fathers died, land of the Pilgrim's pride, From every mountainside, let freedom ring!*

29 And if America is to be a great nation, this must become true.

30 And so let freedom ring from the **prodigious** hilltops of New Hampshire.

31 Let freedom ring from the mighty mountains of New York.

32 Let freedom ring from the heightening Alleghenies of Pennsylvania.

33 Let freedom ring from the snow-capped Rockies of Colorado.

34 Let freedom ring from the curvaceous slopes of California.

35 But not only that:

36 Let freedom ring from Stone Mountain of Georgia.

37 Let freedom ring from Lookout Mountain of Tennessee.

38 Let freedom ring from every hill and molehill of Mississippi.

39 From every mountainside, let freedom ring.

40 And when this happens, and when we allow freedom to ring, when we let it ring from every village and every hamlet, from every state and every city, we will be able to speed up that day when *all* of God's children, black men and white men, Jews and Gentiles, Protestants and Catholics, will be able to join hands and sing in the words of the old Negro spiritual:

41 *Free at last! Free at last!*
Thank God Almighty, we are free at last!

© 1963 Dr. Martin Luther King, Jr. © renewed 1991 Coretta Scott King.

Skill:
Arguments
and Claims

Dr. King has clearly stated that when the audience takes the action he wants them to take, it will lead to a positive outcome. He uses language vividly to describe what will happen if the audience accepts his argument.

First Read

Read "I Have a Dream." After you read, complete the Think Questions below.

☁ THINK QUESTIONS

1. What does Dr. King encourage those who come from persecution to do next? Explain.

2. How does Dr. King address nonviolence in "I Have a Dream"? Cite evidence from the text to support your answer.

3. What does Dr. King say will happen "when we allow freedom to ring"? Give examples.

4. Read the following dictionary entry:

   legitimate le•git•i•mate /ləˈjidəmət/

   adjective

   1. (of a child) born of parents who are lawfully married
   2. ruling by hereditary right
   3. reasonable; able to be defended by logic
   4. lawful; according to the law

   Which definition most closely matches the meaning of **legitimate** as it is used in paragraph 7? Write the correct definition of *legitimate* here and explain how you figured out its meaning.

5. Which context clues helped you determine the meaning of the word **inextricably** as it is used in paragraph 9 of "I Have a Dream"? Write your definition of *inextricably* and indicate the clues that helped you figure out the meaning of the word.

Please note that excerpts and passages in the StudySync® library and this workbook are intended as touchstones to generate interest in an author's work. The excerpts and passages do not substitute for the reading of entire texts, and StudySync® strongly recommends that students seek out and purchase the whole literary or informational work in order to experience it as the author intended. Links to online resellers are available in our digital library. In addition, complete works may be ordered through an authorized reseller by filling out and returning to StudySync® the order form enclosed in this workbook.

Reading & Writing Companion   91

Skill:
Arguments and Claims

Use the Checklist to analyze Arguments and Claims in "I Have a Dream." Refer to the sample student annotations about Arguments and Claims in the text.

••• CHECKLIST FOR ARGUMENTS AND CLAIMS

In order to identify the speaker's argument and claims, note the following:

- ✓ clues that reveal the author's opinion in the title, opening remarks, or concluding statement

- ✓ declarative statements that come before or follow a speaker's anecdote or story

To delineate a speaker's argument and specific claims, do the following:

- ✓ Note the information that the speaker introduces in sequential order.

- ✓ Describe the speaker's argument in your own words.

To evaluate the argument and specific claims, consider the following questions:

- ✓ Does the writer support each claim with reasoning and evidence?

- ✓ Is the reasoning sound and the evidence sufficient?

- ✓ Do the writer's claims work together to support the writer's overall argument?

- ✓ Which claims are not supported, if any?

Skill:
Arguments and Claims

Reread paragraphs 24–29 of "I Have A Dream." Then, using the Checklist on the previous page, answer the multiple-choice questions below.

↻ YOUR TURN

1. Which of the following sentences from the speech directly states an arguable claim?

   ○ A. *"My country 'tis of thee, sweet land of liberty, of thee I sing."*

   ○ B. "And if America is to be a great nation, this must become true."

   ○ C. "This is our hope, and this is the faith that I go back to the South with."

   ○ D. "I have a dream."

2. Which paragraph conveys the *best* example of reasoning?

   ○ A. 10

   ○ B. 18

   ○ C. 21

   ○ D. 28

3. What is another way of stating King's conclusion in paragraphs 27 and 28?

   ○ A. There will come a day when all of God's children will sing.

   ○ B. Everyone in America will be free for one day.

   ○ C. All the people who live in America will truly be free.

   ○ D. People will no longer have to die for freedom.

Please note that excerpts and passages in the StudySync® library and this workbook are intended as touchstones to generate interest in an author's work. The excerpts and passages do not substitute for the reading of entire texts, and StudySync® strongly recommends that students seek out and purchase the whole literary or informational work in order to experience it as the author intended. Links to online resellers are available in our digital library. In addition, complete works may be ordered through an authorized reseller by filling out and returning to StudySync® the order form enclosed in this workbook.

Reading & Writing
Companion

93

Skill:
Rhetoric

Use the Checklist to analyze Rhetoric in "I Have a Dream." Refer to the sample student annotations about Rhetoric in the text.

••• CHECKLIST FOR RHETORIC

In order to identify an author's or speaker's point of view or purpose in a text, note the following:

- ✓ the purpose of the text

- ✓ details and statements that identify the author's or speaker's point of view or purpose

- ✓ when an author or speaker may be objective or biased

- ✓ when the author or speaker uses rhetorical devices to advance a purpose or a specific point of view. Rhetoric refers to the persuasive use of language in a text or speech, such as:

    - • logical reasoning, supported by evidence, facts, or statistics

    - • an emotional plea by personalizing a situation or occurrence

    - • reminding readers or listeners of their shared values and beliefs

To determine an author's or speaker's point of view or purpose in a text and analyze how an author or speaker uses rhetoric, consider the following questions:

- ✓ Does the author or speaker employ rhetoric in the text? If so, what kind?

- ✓ How does the writer or speaker try to persuade readers? Are there any emotional pleas meant to evoke sympathy, or does the author or speaker only present facts and statistics?

- ✓ How does the writer's or speaker's use of rhetoric reveal his or her purpose for writing or speaking?

- ✓ What does the use of rhetoric disclose about the author's or speaker's point of view toward the subject?

To analyze the purpose of the rhetorical devices used in the text, use the following questions as a guide:

- ✓ How does this argument use rhetorical devices to persuade an audience?

- ✓ What is the purpose of certain rhetorical devices in this text or speech?

Skill:
Rhetoric

Reread paragraphs 26–39 of "I Have A Dream." Then, using the Checklist on the previous page, answer the multiple-choice questions below.

↻ YOUR TURN

1. This question has two parts. First, answer Part A. Then, answer Part B.

   Part A: What purpose is King trying to achieve through his use of rhetoric in his speech?

   ○ A. King uses rhetoric as an appeal to logic, which is illustrated through the way in which he cites evidence.

   ○ B. King uses rhetoric to join opposing ideas in order to appeal to the audience's emotions and show conflict between opposing values.

   ○ C. King uses rhetoric to draw on shared beliefs and celebrate that America is already a land of liberty and freedom.

   ○ D. King uses rhetoric to appeal to the audience's emotions by describing what the future could be like if true equality was achieved.

   Part B: What evidence best supports King's use of rhetoric to achieve the purpose identified in Part A?

   ○ A. "With this faith, we will be able to work together, to pray together, to struggle together, to go to jail together, to stand up for freedom together, knowing that we will be free one day."

   ○ B. "Let freedom ring from the mighty mountains of New York. Let freedom ring from the heightening Alleghenies of Pennsylvania."

   ○ C. "And this will be the day — this will be the day when all of God's children will be able to sing with new meaning"

   ○ D. *"My country 'tis of thee, sweet land of liberty, of thee I sing. Land where my fathers died, land of the Pilgrim's pride, From every mountainside, let freedom ring!"*

Please note that excerpts and passages in the StudySync® library and this workbook are intended as touchstones to generate interest in an author's work. The excerpts and passages do not substitute for the reading of entire texts, and StudySync® strongly recommends that students seek out and purchase the whole literary or informational work in order to experience it as the author intended. Links to online resellers are available in our digital library. In addition, complete works may be ordered through an authorized reseller by filling out and returning to StudySync® the order form enclosed in this workbook.

Reading & Writing
Companion

95

Close Read

Reread "I Have a Dream." As you reread, complete the Skills Focus questions below. Then use your answers and annotations from the questions to help you complete the Write activity.

◎ SKILLS FOCUS

1. Highlight examples of antithesis and parallelism that King uses to demonstrate the failure of the Emancipation Proclamation to fulfill its promise to people of color. Identify what King is contrasting, what is being repeated, and explain how these rhetorical devices make the speech more persuasive.

2. Highlight King's use of an extended metaphor to support his claim that the United States has failed to live up to the promises made in the Declaration of Independence and the Constitution. Identify the two things are being compared and explain how this extended metaphor enhances King's argument.

3. Highlight a passage in which King uses evidence to support his claim that African Americans need to keep fighting against discrimination and

segregation. Identify King's intended audience for this claim and evidence and how the evidence enhances his argument.

4. "Welcome to America" and "I Have a Dream" explore how a group of people encounter injustices because of their ethnic or racial identities. Identify a passage in "I Have a Dream" in which King identifies the injustices that people of color have met in the United States. Write an annotation that compares these injustices to the injustices faced by Syrian refugees in the United States, as depicted in "Welcome to America."

5. Highlight a section in paragraphs 15–19 in which King uses a rhetorical appeal to support his claim. In your annotation, explain what the rhetorical appeal is and what conclusion he wants his listeners to draw.

✎ WRITE

ARGUMENTATIVE: What evidence, appeals, and rhetorical techniques does King utilize to support and enhance his claim that the promises made in the Declaration of Independence, the Constitution, and the Emancipation Proclamation have not been kept with regard to people of color?

Copyright © BookheadEd Learning, LLC

The Future in My Arms

INFORMATIONAL TEXT
Edwidge Danticat
2002

Introduction

Haitian American writer Edwidge Danticat (b. 1969) is known for her authentic portrayal of Haitian culture in which she emphasizes women's experiences and the search for a collective national identity. Many of her works are based, at least in part, on her own life and cultural history—such as her 1995 collection of short stories, *Krik? Krak!*, and 1998's *Farming of Bones*, a work of historical fiction. In "The Future in My Arms," Danticat relives the events and feelings

"May your arms always be a repozwa, a place where a child can rest her head . . ."

1   I had never held any living thing so tiny in my hands. Six pounds and one ounce, lighter than my smallest dumbbell was my newborn niece, her face bright pink, her eyes tightly shut, her body coiled around itself in a fetal position, still **defiantly** resisting the world into which she'd just been thrust. I had been awaiting her birth with feverish **anticipation**; I was going away for the summer, and I didn't want to leave before she was born, only to come back eight weeks later and find that she had grown **accustomed** to most things in the world except her auntie on her father's side, the sole woman child in a family of men, who all her life had dreamed of having a sister.

2   She arrived the day before I was to leave. I was at the Brooklyn Public Library researching an article when I called to check my messages. In a breathless voice, my brother Andre announced, "You are now the proud aunt of Nadira Amahs Danticat. Her name means, 'She who God has chosen.'"

3   I ran out of the library and headed toward a flower shop on Flatbush Avenue. As I approached, I heard someone call out my name. It was my brother Karl and Mia, who were expecting their own child in a few months. They, too, were heading to the hospital to see Nadira.

4   On the way there, I remembered a message that a girlfriend of mine, a new mother, had sent me for my thirtieth birthday a few months before. "May your arms always be a **repozwa**, a place where a child can rest her head," it said. I had told her that two of my brothers were becoming fathers, and she wanted me to share those words with them. But I'd decided to wait until both my niece and nephew were born to share this with their parents—that we had each become a repozwa, the Haitian Creole[1] term for "sacred place," in whose **shelter** children would now seek rest.

5   By the time we got to the hospital, my sister-in-law, Carol, had already had a few visitors. She appeared exhausted but in good spirits as she and Andre took us down the corridor to the maternity-ward window. Which one was

---

1. **Haitian Creole** a language derived from a mixture of French and African languages originally spoken by enslaved peoples

Nadira? Andre wanted us to guess, to pick her out of the rows of infants like a long-lost relative in a crowd of strangers. We were aided in our task by the small pink name tag glued to her bassinet. Carol asked if we wanted to have a closer look. We went back to the room and waited for the nurse to bring her in.

6   We all stood up when she was carried in. I knew I was getting ahead of myself, but this made me think of a wedding where everyone immediately—and almost instinctively—rises to greet the bride. She was passed from loving hand to loving hand, but I kept her longer. I would soon have to leave, so I wanted to hold her, to cradle her in my arms, let her tiny head rest in the crook of my elbow. I wanted to watch her ever so slightly open her eyes and tighten her mouth as she battled to make sense of all the new sounds around her, all the laughter, the wild comparisons with relatives living and gone, all so very present in her face. I wanted to read her lines from Sonia Sanchez's "Poem at Thirty": "i am here waiting / remembering that / once as a child / i walked two / miles in my sleep. / did i know / then where i / was going? / traveling. i'm always traveling. / i want to tell / you about me. . . / here is my hand."

7   Nadira's presence had already transformed the room. Her opening her eyes was like a Hollywood press conference, with all the video and picture cameras going off, trying to capture something that perhaps none of us knew how to express, that we had suddenly been allowed a closer view of one of life's great wonders, and by being there, were an extension of a miracle that happened every second of every day in every part of the world, but had generously now granted us a turn.

8   That day, when we lined up for a glance, a touch, a picture, and tried to imagine a life for Nadira in a new country, we each made our own silent promises not to let her face that new world alone. We were telling her and her parents that we were her village with our offers of baby-sitting favors, our giant teddy bears, our handfuls of flowers, and the crooks of our arms and necks and laps, which we hoped that she would run to if she ever needed a refuge.

9   Looking back on my own thirty years, having crossed many borders, loved and lost my family and friends, young and old, to time, migrations, illnesses, I couldn't help but worry for Nadira, and for my nephew yet to be born. Are there ahead for them wars, a depression, a holocaust, a new civil-rights struggle as there were for those children born at the dawn of the last century? Will they have to face the colonization of new planets, genetic cloning, new forms of slavery, and other nightmares we have yet to imagine? Will we, their tiny village, give them enough love and assurance to help them survive, thrive, and even want to challenge those things?

10   Before handing Nadira back to her parents, I felt torn between wanting her to grow up quickly so that her body might match the wits she'd need to face her future and at the same time wanting her to stay small so that she might be easier to shield and carry along the length of our elbows to the reach of our palms. I wanted to tell her parents that though I had never held any living thing so tiny in my hands, I had never held anything so grand either, a bundle so elaborately complex and yet fragile, encompassing both our past and our future.

11   Though Nadira and my soon-to-arrive nephew were not created specifically with me in mind, I felt as though they were the most magical gifts that could have ever blessed my thirtieth year of life. Humbled by my responsibility to them, I silently promised their parents that for the next thirty years and the thirty after that, my heart and soul would be their children's repozwa, a sacred place where they would always find rest.

[The author's nephew, Karl William Ezekial Danticat, was born on August 23, 1999.]

First published in Ebony and reprinted by permission of Edwidge Danticat and Aragi Inc.

✏ WRITE

PERSONAL RESPONSE: Write a letter to a sibling, friend, neighbor, or fellow student to whom you are a leader, role model, or caregiver. In the letter, describe how someone's presence in your life helped you achieve a sense of belonging. Then, describe how you hope to nurture a similar feeling in this other young person by virtue of your support and guidance. As part of your letter, describe how your experiences or hopes parallel Danticat's.

Extended Writing Project and Grammar

EXTENDED WRITING PROJECT

NARRATIVE WRITING

Narrative Writing Process: Plan

PLAN	DRAFT	REVISE	EDIT AND PUBLISH

"No man is an island," John Donne wrote nearly 400 years ago. Today, as well as back then, his metaphor highlights the important role that belonging plays in the human experience. But belonging is not always easy. It can be a struggle to find a group that accepts us for who we are. Being a member of one group can put us at odds with members of another group, and the groups we belong to in our youth may limit us later in life.

WRITING PROMPT

How does belonging or not belonging in a group affect our sense of self?

Use what you have learned in this unit to create a real or imagined narrative that shows how belonging or not belonging in a group affects a person at an important life moment.

Identify a person who identifies as a member of a group, or who is trying to become part of one. This person may be you, based on your personal experience, or a fictional character whom you invent. Develop a plan for your narrative in which this person faces a conflict because of his or her identity. Include in your plan pivotal moments that show how the group's response (supportive? unsupportive? welcoming? indifferent?) affects the resolution of the person's conflict, either positively or negatively. Use your plan to write your narrative, remembering to include the following:

- a well-developed protagonist and other characters
- a plot that includes pivotal moments
- a distinct conflict and resolution
- a clear setting
- dialogue and description
- a thoughtful theme or reflection connected to the prompt

Copyright © BookheadEd Learning, LLC

Introduction to Narrative Writing

Narrative writing is a genre in which a writer creates a story out of real or imagined events. A narrative is usually organized by the plot, or the series of events that take place in a story. The plot is driven by a conflict, or a problem that the characters face. It is presented by a narrator, who tells the story in the first person (as a participant) or in the third person (as an outside observer). The narrator also reveals how the author develops the characters.

When organizing a narrative, first orient the reader by providing background information about the characters and the setting. Then create an inciting incident. This is an event that pushes a character into the main action of the story, one that will lead to the problem the character must solve. The events that lead to a solution should unfold naturally and logically, as in a series of cause and effect relationships.

As you continue with this Extended Writing Project, you'll receive more instruction and practice at crafting each of the characteristics of fiction writing to create your own real or imagined narrative.

Before you get started on your own real or imagined narrative, read this personal narrative that one student, Mason, wrote in response to the writing prompt. As you read the Model, highlight and annotate the features of narrative writing that Mason included in his narrative.

NOTES

≡ STUDENT MODEL

They Call Me "Clicks"

1   I don't actually remember how I got the scar on my face. I was pretty small at the time. I think I fell against a glass table. It's less noticeable now, but it's still impressive. It looks like a couple of lightning bolts on my left cheek, and it would look cool on a superhero but not so much on a skinny teenager. I stopped asking my dad about it a long time ago because he'd always get this weird look on his face, like he might get sick. He probably did feel sick remembering the worst day of his life when he had to watch his kid's face get sewn back together. I barely even notice the scar, but that's usually the first thing people see when we meet. And I meet a lot of people because we move around a lot because my mom is in the military. By seventh grade, I got tired of having to tell the story of how I got my scar every time I met somebody new. For a while I'd play dumb. If they asked, I'd say, "What scar?" But people thought I was socially awkward at best or a sarcastic jerk at worst. Then I tried shrugging and saying, "I don't remember" and kept moving. I'd leave it up to other people to come up with exciting stories about my face on their own. As a result, I didn't really fit in.

2   Then last year, my mom brought me this cool camera from when she was stationed in Japan. It takes way better pictures than my phone. I started taking it to school events like basketball games and track meets and school plays. Behind a camera, I could be at school with the other kids without having to be "the kid with the ugly scar." I got up close to the action and clicked pictures. I showed them to the yearbook and the school newspaper staff, and people loved them. I started carrying my camera everywhere. It was like wearing an invisibility cloak. It allowed me to finally feel like I fit in at school and in the community. I didn't have to explain who I was or why I was there or where my scar came from.

3   One day I was taking pictures at school, and I caught a glimpse of my reflection in a window. All I could see was my big head of curly hair

and the camera where my face should be. It made me wonder if maybe the reason nobody bothered to ask me about my scar anymore wasn't because I fit in but because I always had a camera in front of my face. Something felt wrong about that. So, I decided to give myself a test.

4   The class picnic was coming up. I decided to go but for once to leave my precious camera at home! Without the weight of the camera around my neck, I felt exposed. I put on a ball cap, and that made me feel a little more like myself, but you could still see my face. At the picnic, I sat near kids I knew from the newspaper, and I talked to some of my teachers, and that was fine. Then I tried to join a game of softball. That's when I got into trouble. Jimmy, a kid from the basketball team, came up to me and said, "Dude, this game is only for kids who go to our school." I looked around nervously. I said, "I do go to our school." Jimmy shook his head. He said, "I know everybody in our grade, and I don't know you." He seemed to be getting angry.

5   Suddenly the girl standing next to him, Clarice, said, "Wait! Jimmy, he *does* go to our school. He's Clicks!"

6   *Clicks?*

7   Jimmy looked at me more closely. "You're the kid with the camera? The one who's always taking pictures of the basketball games? My mom, she really loved that picture you took of me making the winning shot. Nice!" He held out his fist, and I tapped it with mine.

8   A big sigh of relief escaped my lips. It turned out that I wasn't going to get beat up, and I had a nickname that was kind of cool. Who knew? All this time, people had been thinking of me not as that kid with the scar but as the kid with the camera. Maybe I wasn't such an outsider after all.

9   Next thing I knew, Jimmy and Clarice were asking me to take their picture with her phone. Then we took a selfie, and Clarice sent it to me. And then we all played some softball. I probably missed some action shots during the game, but for once I didn't care. For once, I was in the game, not just observing it, and that felt pretty good.

Please note that excerpts and passages in the StudySync® library and this workbook are intended as touchstones to generate interest in an author's work. The excerpts and passages do not substitute for the reading of entire texts, and StudySync® strongly recommends that students seek out and purchase the whole literary or informational work in order to experience it as the author intended. Links to online resellers are available in our digital library. In addition, complete works may be ordered through an authorized reseller by filling out and returning to StudySync® the order form enclosed in this workbook.

Reading & Writing Companion   105

✎ WRITE

Writers often take notes about story ideas before they sit down to write. Think about what you've learned so far about narrative writing to help you begin prewriting.

- **Purpose**: What conflict related to belonging do you want to write about? Will it be one you yourself have experienced, or will you invent one?

- **Audience**: Who is your audience and what message do you want to express to your audience?

- **Characters**: Will you write about yourself, or a made-up character? What group made up of other characters will play a role in the story?

- **Plot**: What events will lead to the resolution of the conflict while keeping a reader engaged?

- **Setting**: How might the setting of your story affect the characters and conflict?

- **Theme/Reflection**: If you are writing an imagined narrative, what general message about life do you want to express? If you are writing a real narrative, what careful thoughts about the significance of your experience will you include?

- **Point of View**: From which point of view should your story be told, and why?

Response Instructions

Use the questions in the bulleted list to write a one-paragraph summary. Your summary should describe what will happen in your narrative.

Don't worry about including all of the details now; focus only on the most essential and important elements. You will refer to this short summary as you continue through the steps of the writing process.

Skill:
Organizing Narrative Writing

••• CHECKLIST FOR ORGANIZING NARRATIVE WRITING

As you consider how to organize your writing for your narrative, use the following questions as a guide:

- Who is the narrator and who are the characters in the story?
- Will the story be told from one or multiple points of view?
- Where will the story take place?
- What conflict or problem will the characters have to resolve?
- Have I created a smooth progression of experiences or plot events?

Here are some strategies to help you create a smooth progression of experiences or events in your narrative:

- Establish a context

  > choose a setting and a situation, problem, or observation that characters will have to face and resolve

  > use cause-and-effect relationships or a sequential structure to create a smooth progression of experiences or events

  > decide how the conflict will be be resolved

    o the problem often builds to a climax, when the characters are forced to take action

- Introduce a narrator and/or characters

  > characters can be introduced all at once or over the course of the narrative

  > choose the role each character will play in the story

  > choose one or multiple points of view, either first or third person

    o a first-person narrator can be a participant or character in the story

    o a third-person narrator tells the story as an outside observer

⟳ YOUR TURN

Complete the chart below by matching each event to its correct place in the narrative sequence.

	Event Options
A	He figures out he has to stay in the new world.
B	The main character wakes up in a dark room.
C	He realizes the new world is similar to his old one, and he can be happy there.
D	He tries to find a way home, but is unable to.
E	He doesn't see anything familiar, but he decides to walk around and figure out where he is.

Narrative Sequence	Event
Exposition	
Rising Action	
Climax	
Falling Action	
Resolution	

⟳ YOUR TURN

Complete the chart below by writing a short summary of what will happen in each section of your narrative.

Narrative Sequence	Event
Exposition	
Rising Action	
Climax	
Falling Action	
Resolution	

Narrative Writing Process: Draft

| PLAN | DRAFT | REVISE | EDIT AND PUBLISH |

You have already made progress toward writing your real or imagined narrative. Now it is time to draft your real or imagined narrative.

✏ WRITE

Use your plan and other responses in your Binder to draft your narrative. You may also have new ideas as you begin drafting. Feel free to explore those new ideas as you have them. You can also ask yourself these questions to ensure that your writing is focused, organized, and detailed:

Draft Checklist:

☐ **Focus**: Have I made the conflict clear to readers? Have I included only relevant information and details and nothing extraneous that might confuse my readers?

☐ **Organization**: Does the sequence of events in my story make sense? Will readers be engaged by the organization and want to keep reading to find out what happens next?

☐ **Ideas and Details**: Does my writing flow together naturally, or is it choppy? Will my readers be able to easily follow and understand descriptions of characters, settings, or events?

Before you submit your draft, read it over carefully. You want to be sure that you've responded to all aspects of the prompt.

Please note that excerpts and passages in the StudySync® library and this workbook are intended as touchstones to generate interest in an author's work. The excerpts and passages do not substitute for the reading of entire texts, and StudySync® strongly recommends that students seek out and purchase the whole literary or informational work in order to experience it as the author intended. Links to online resellers are available in our digital library. In addition, complete works may be ordered through an authorized reseller by filling out and returning to StudySync® the order form enclosed in this workbook.

Reading & Writing Companion **109**

Here is Mason's narrative draft. As you read, notice how Mason develops his draft to be focused, detailed, and organized. As Mason continues to revise and edit his narrative, he will find and improve weak spots in his writing, as well as correct any language or punctuation mistakes.

STUDENT MODEL: FIRST DRAFT

 Skill:
Story Beginnings

Mason improves his narrative's beginning by including a surprising statement as his opening sentence. This not only helps readers learn about the main character but also about a source of conflict.

 Skill:
Narrative Techniques

Mason wants his readers to understand why the scar presents an obstacle to fitting in. He uses details to describe the scar and reflect on how traumatic the accident was.

They Call Me "Clicks"

~~I was pretty small at the time. I think I fell against a glass table. It's less noticable now, but it's still impressive. I barely even notice the scar, but that's usually the first thing people saw when we meet. By seventh grade, I got tired of having to tell the story of how I got my scar every time I met somebody new. For a while I'd play dumb. If they asked, I'd say, "What scar?" But people thought I was socially awkward at best or a sarcastic jerk at worst. Then I tried shruging and saying, "I don't remember" and kept moving. I'd leave it up to other people to come up with exciting stories about my face on their own.~~

I don't actually remember how I got the scar on my face. I was pretty small at the time. I think I fell against a glass table. It's less noticeable now, but it's still impressive. It looks like a couple of lightning bolts on my left cheek, and it would look cool on a superhero but not so much on a skinny teenager. I stopped asking my dad about it a long time ago because he'd always get this weird look on his face, like he might get sick. He probably did feel sick remembering the worst day of his life when he had to watch his kid's face get sewn back together. I barely even notice the scar, but that's usually the first thing people see when we meet. And I meet a lot of people because we move around a lot because my mom is in the military. By seventh grade, I got tired of having to tell the story of how I got my scar every time I met somebody new. For a while I'd play dumb. If they asked, I'd say, "What scar?" But people thought I was socially awkward at best or a sarcastic jerk at worst. Then I tried shrugging and saying, "I don't remember" and kept moving. I'd leave it up to other people to come up with exciting stories about my face on their own. As a result, I didn't really fit in.

Then last year, my mom brought me this cool camera from when she was stationed in Japan. It takes way better pictures than my phone. I started taking it to school events like basketball games and track

NOTES

meets and school plays. Behind a camera, I could be at school with the other kids without having to be "the kid with the ugly scar." It was like wearing an invisable cloak. It allowed me to finally feel like I fit in at school. And in the community. I didn't have to explain who I was or why I was there or where my scar came from.

~~One day I was taking pictures at school, and I saw my reflection. All I could see was my head and the camera. It made me wonder. Maybe the reason nobody bothered to ask me about my scar anymore wasn't because I fit in. Maybe it was because I always had a camera in front of my face. Something felt wrong about that. So, I decided to give myself a test.~~

One day I was taking pictures at school, and I caught a glimpse of my reflection in a window. All I could see was my big head of curly hair and the camera where my face should be. It made me wonder. Maybe the reason nobody bothered to ask me about my scar anymore wasn't because I fit in. Maybe it was because I always had a camera in front of my face. Something felt wrong about that. So, I decided to give myself a test.

~~The class picnic was coming up. I decided to go but for once to leave my precious camera at home! Without the wieght of the camera around my neck, I felt exposed. I put on a ball cap, and that made me feel a little more like myself. Still see my face. At the picnic, I sit near kids I knew from the newspaper, and I talked to some of my teachers, and that was fine. Then I tried to join a game of softball. That's when I got into trouble. Jimmy, a kid from the basketball team, comes up to me and said, "Dude, this game is only for kids who go to our school." I looked around nervously? I said, "I do go to our school." Jimmy shook his head. He said, "I know everybody in our grade, and I don't know you." He seemed to be geting angry.~~

The class picnic was coming up. I decided to go but for once to leave my precious camera at home. Without the weight of the camera around my neck, I felt exposed. I put on a ball cap, and that made me feel a little more like myself, but you could still see my face. At the picnic, I sat near kids I knew from the newspaper, and I talked to some of my teachers, and that was fine. Then I tried to join a game of softball. That's when I got into trouble. Jimmy, a kid from the basketball team, came up to me and said, "Dude, this game is only

Skill:
Descriptive Details

Mason adds details to make his narration more appealing to his readers' sense of sight. He wants to use precise language, such as specific nouns and action verbs to better describe the setting and his appearance and state of mind.

Skill:
Narrative Sequencing Climax

At the picnic, Mason doesn't bring his camera, sits near kids he knows from the newspaper, and talks to teachers. When he tries to join a softball game, he gets into trouble. Jimmy doesn't recognize him and seems angry.

for kids who go to our school." I looked around nervously. I said, "I do go to our school." Jimmy shook his head. He said, "I know everybody in our grade, and I don't know you." He seemed to be getting angry.

The girl standing next to him looked at me thoughtfully. I could tell she was running through her memory bank trying to place me.

"Oh, yeah! You're Clicks," the girl said.

"You're the kid with the camera? The one who's always taking pictures of the basketball games? My mom, she really loved that picture you took of me making the winning shot. Nice!" He held out his fist, and I tapped it with mine.

A big sigh of relief escaped my lips. I had a nickname that was kind of cool. Who knew? And I wasn't going to get beat up! All this time, people had been thinking of me not as that kid with the scar but as the kid with the camera. Maybe I wasn't such an outsider after all.

Next thing I knew, Jimmy and Clarice were asking me to take their picture with her phone. Then we took a selfie, and Clarice sent it to me. And then we all played some softball. I probably missed some action shots during the game, but for once I didn't care. For once, I was in the game, not just observing it, and that felt pretty good.

**Skill:
Conclusion**

Mason thinks about how he can further develop the resolution of the conflict and leave readers with a lasting impression about the character. He wants to show how the other student recognizing "Clicks" leads to other changes, including what "Clicks" believes about himself.

Skill:
Story Beginnings

••• CHECKLIST FOR STORY BEGINNINGS

Before you write the beginning of your narrative, ask yourself the following questions:

- What information does my reader need to know at the beginning of the story about the narrator, main character, setting, and the character's conflict?

- What will happen to my character in the story?

- Who is the narrator of my story? Should I establish either a singular narrator or multiple points of view?

There are many ways to help you engage and orient your reader. Here are some methods to help you set out a problem, situation, or observation, establish one or multiple point(s) of view, and introduce a narrator and/or characters:

- Action

  > What action could help reveal information about my character or conflict?

  > How might an exciting moment grab my reader's attention?

  > How could a character's reaction or observation help set the mood?

- Description

  > Does my story take place in a special location or specific time period?

  > How can describing a location or character grab my readers' attention? What powerful emotions can I use?

- Dialogue

  > What dialogue would help my reader understand the setting or the conflict?

  > How could a character's internal thoughts provide information for my reader?

- Information

  > Would a surprising statement grab readers' attention?

  > What details will help my reader understand the character, conflict, or setting?

- Point of view

  > one point of view: first person, third person, third-person omniscient, or third-person limited

  > multiple points of view, introducing more than one narrator or character to tell the story

Please note that excerpts and passages in the StudySync® library and this workbook are intended as touchstones to generate interest in an author's work. The excerpts and passages do not substitute for the reading of entire texts, and StudySync® strongly recommends that students seek out and purchase the whole literary or informational work in order to experience it as the author intended. Links to online resellers are available in our digital library. In addition, complete works may be ordered through an authorized reseller by filling out and returning to StudySync® the order form enclosed in this workbook.

Reading & Writing Companion   113

YOUR TURN

Choose the best answer to each question.

1. Below is a section from a previous draft of Mason's story. The meaning of the underlined sentences is unclear. Which sentence can be added to the beginning to help clarify the meaning?

> <u>I was pretty small at the time. I think I fell against a glass table. It's less noticable now, but it's still impressive.</u> I barely even notice the scar, but that's usually the first thing people saw when we meet. And I meet a lot of people because we move around a lot. My mom is in the military.

- ○ A. When I was 5 years old I began to read.
- ○ B. I don't actually remember how I got the scar on my face.
- ○ C. Once upon a time something interesting happened.
- ○ D. There are many reasons why I don't fit in.

2. Mason wants to improve the beginning of a previous draft of his story. Which sentence(s) would give more expository information about the character and his conflict, if inserted after the underlined sentence?

> <u>I barely even notice the scar, but that's usually the first thing people saw when we meet.</u> By seventh grade, I got tired of having to tell the story of how I got my scar every time I met somebody new.

- ○ A. And I just continue to explain myself.
- ○ B. Everyone would just look at me strangely and then ask the question.
- ○ C. I've met so many people since I was a young child.
- ○ D. And I meet a lot of people because we move around a lot. My mom is in the military.

 WRITE

Use the questions in the checklist section to revise the beginning of your narrative.

Skill:
Narrative Techniques

••• CHECKLIST FOR NARRATIVE TECHNIQUES

As you begin to develop the techniques you will use in your narrative, ask yourself the following questions:

- Is it clear which character is talking in a dialogue?

- Is the pacing of events suitable and effective?

- Which literary devices can strengthen descriptions of the characters or plot events? How can I use personal reflection to develop my narrative?

- What additional characters and/or events might help to develop the narrative?

Here are some methods that can help you write dialogue, pacing, description, reflection, and multiple plot lines, to develop experiences, events, and/or characters in your narrative:

- use character dialogue to explain events or actions

  > use quotation marks correctly

  > include identifying names as needed before or after quotation marks

- use description so the reader can visualize the characters, setting, and other elements

  > descriptions should contribute to the reader's understanding of the element being described.

- use pacing effectively

  > for a quick pace, use limited description, short paragraphs, brief dialogue, and simpler sentences

  > for a slower place, use detailed description, longer paragraphs, and complex sentence structures

- use reflection to comment on the overall message

  > include character or personal inner thoughts or personal insight

- create multiple plot lines that further develop the narrative's message

  > include characters, events, or other elements that will further develop the plot

- use any combination of the techniques above

YOUR TURN

Choose the best answer to each question.

1. Mason wants to improve the ending of a previous draft of his narrative. Which sentence could he add to provide more reflection about the significance of his experience?

> All this time, people had been thinking of me not as that kid with the scar but as the kid with the camera.

- ○ A. Who knew?
- ○ B. I really needed to improve my photography skills.
- ○ C. Maybe I wasn't such an outsider after all.
- ○ D. I was so relieved!

2. Mason wants to improve the ending of a previous draft of his narrative. How can he rewrite the underlined sentence to provide more reflection about the significance of the events?

> I probably missed some action shots during the game, but for once I didn't care. <u>For once, I felt pretty good.</u>

- ○ A. For once, I didn't feel bad about myself.
- ○ B. For once, I was in the game, not just observing it, and that felt pretty good.
- ○ C. For once, it didn't matter.
- ○ D. For once, I wasn't worried about action shots.

 WRITE

Use the questions in the checklist to revise your narrative using narrative techniques.

Skill:
Narrative Sequencing

••• CHECKLIST FOR NARRATIVE SEQUENCING

As you develop the series of events in your narrative, ask yourself the following questions:

- What important background information could I add to the exposition?
- How could I make the conflict in my story clearer?
- Did I provide a clear point of view, or include multiple points of view?
- Do the events of the rising action, climax, falling action, and resolution flow smoothly?
- What other techniques could I use so that events in my story build on one another, creating a coherent whole?
- How can I tie together the events of my story to conclude it?

Here are some strategies that can help you use a variety of techniques to sequence events so that they build on one another to create a coherent whole:

- identify the main conflict of your story and how it will be resolved
- establish one or more points of view
- for the exposition, identify the important background information your readers should know about the setting, characters, and conflict
- outline the events that will be part of the rising action, climax, falling action, and resolution
- sequence events so they build to create a coherent whole by:

  > foreshadowing, or giving hints about what is going to happen

  > establishing character traits and habits before presenting the character with a difficult choice

Please note that excerpts and passages in the StudySync® library and this workbook are intended as touchstones to generate interest in an author's work. The excerpts and passages do not substitute for the reading of entire texts, and StudySync® strongly recommends that students seek out and purchase the whole literary or informational work in order to experience it as the author intended. Links to online resellers are available in our digital library. In addition, complete works may be ordered through an authorized reseller by filling out and returning to StudySync® the order form enclosed in this workbook.

Reading & Writing Companion

117

YOUR TURN

Complete the chart below by matching each event to its correct place in the narrative sequence.

	Event Options
A	The main character moves to a new town and starts going to a new school. She is very shy, but she loves to draw.
B	The two girls realize they have a lot in common and become friends.
C	There is a tense moment when another girl confronts the main character for sitting at her usual table in the library.
D	The other girl notices the main character's drawings in her notebook, and compliments her on them.
E	She is too shy to ask to sit with the other kids at lunch, so she eats by herself in the library.

Narrative Sequence	Event
Exposition	
Rising Action	
Climax	
Falling Action	
Resolution	

YOUR TURN

Complete the chart below by writing a short summary of what will happen in each section of your narrative.

Narrative Sequence	Event
Exposition	
Rising Action	
Climax	
Falling Action	
Resolution	

Skill:
Descriptive Details

sync•skills

••• CHECKLIST FOR DESCRIPTIVE DETAILS

First, reread the draft of your narrative and identify the following:

- where descriptive details are needed to convey experiences and events
- vague, general, or overused words and phrases
- places where you want to tell how something looks, sounds, feels, smells, or tastes, such as:

  > experiences

  > events

  > settings

  > characters

Use precise words and phrases, telling details, and sensory language to convey a vivid picture of the experiences, events, setting, and/or characters, using the following questions as a guide:

- What experiences and events do I want to convey in my writing?
- Have I included telling details that help reveal the experiences and events in the story?
- How do I want the characters and setting portrayed?
- How can I use sensory language, or words that describe sights, sounds, feels, smells, or tastes, so that readers can clearly visualize the experiences, events, setting, and/or characters in my story?
- What can I refine or revise in my word choice to make sure that the reader can picture what is taking place?

Please note that excerpts and passages in the StudySync® library and this workbook are intended as touchstones to generate interest in an author's work. The excerpts and passages do not substitute for the reading of entire texts, and StudySync® strongly recommends that students seek out and purchase the whole literary or informational work in order to experience it as the author intended. Links to online resellers are available in our digital library. In addition, complete works may be ordered through an authorized reseller by filling out and returning to StudySync® the order form enclosed in this workbook.

Reading & Writing
Companion

119

⟳ YOUR TURN

Choose the best answer to each question.

1. Below is a section from a previous draft of Mason's story. Mason wants to add a descriptive sight detail to the underlined sentence. Which sentence best adds sight detail to this sentence?

> When I was taking photos, I was no longer "the kid with the ugly scar." I could get close to the action, and no one noticed me. <u>My camera hid my face</u>.

○ A. My camera drew attention away from my face.
○ B. My camera was like a cloak of invisibility.
○ C. My camera was like a clear mask.
○ D. My camera obscured my scar.

2. Below is a section from a previous draft of Mason's story. Mason wants to revise the underlined sentence using sound details. Which sentence best accomplishes this goal?

> <u>I was relieved.</u> It turned out that Jimmy wasn't going to beat me up, and I even had a cool nickname.

○ A. I sighed inwardly.
○ B. My face muscles relaxed in relief.
○ C. A big sigh of relief escaped my lips.
○ D. Inwardly, I felt the stress melt away.

✏ WRITE

Use the questions in the checklist to revise your narrative.

Skill: Conclusions

••• CHECKLIST FOR CONCLUSIONS

Before you write your conclusion, ask yourself the following questions:

- What important details should I include in the summary in my conclusion?

- What other thoughts and feelings could the characters share with readers in the conclusion?

- Should I express the importance of the events in my narrative through dialogue or a character's actions?

Below are two strategies to help you provide a conclusion that follows from and reflects on what is experienced, observed, or resolved over the course of the narrative:

- Peer Discussion

  > After you have written your introduction and body paragraphs, talk with a partner about possible endings for your narrative, writing notes about your discussion.

  > Review your notes and think about how you want to end your story.

  > Briefly summarize the events in the narrative through the narrator or one of the characters.

  > Describe the narrator's observations about the events they experienced.

  > Reveal to readers why the experiences in the narrative matter through a character's reflections or resolutions.

  > Write your conclusion.

- Freewriting

  > Freewrite for 10 minutes about what you might include in your conclusion. Don't worry about grammar, punctuation, or having fully formed ideas. The point of freewriting is to discover ideas.

  > Review your notes and think about how you want to end your story.

  > Briefly summarize the events in the narrative through the narrator or one of the characters.

  > Describe the narrator's observations about the events they experienced.

  > Reveal to readers why the experiences in the narrative matter through a character's reflections or resolutions.

  > Write your conclusion.

Reading & Writing Companion   **121**

YOUR TURN

Choose the best answer to each question.

1. Below is a section from a previous draft of Mason's story. Which sentence best reveals the characters' acceptance of Mason at the end?

> "You're the kid with the camera? The one who's always taking pictures of the basketball games? My mom, she really loved that picture you took of me making the winning shot. Nice!" He held out his fist, and I tapped it with mine.

- ○ A. You're the kid with the camera?
- ○ B. He held out his fist, and I tapped it with mine.
- ○ C. The one who's always taking pictures of the basketball games?
- ○ D. My mom, she really loved that picture you took of me making the winning shot.

2. Read the section below. Which sentence is used to emphasize the significance of the change that took place for "Clicks"?

> Next thing I knew, Jimmy and Clarice were asking me to take their picture with her phone. Then we took a selfie, and Clarice sent it to me. And then we all played some softball. I probably missed some action shots during the game, but for once I didn't care. For once! I was in the game, not just observing it, and that felt pretty good.

- ○ A. Next thing I knew, Jimmy and Clarice were asking me to take their picture with her phone.
- ○ B. Then we took a selfie, and Clarice sent it to me.
- ○ C. And then we all played some softball.
- ○ D. I probably missed some action shots during the game, but for once I didn't care.

 WRITE

Use the questions in the checklist section to revise the conclusion of your narrative so that it follows logically from the events of the plot and what the characters have experienced.

Narrative Writing Process: Revise

PLAN	DRAFT	REVISE	EDIT AND PUBLISH

You have written a draft of your real or imagined narrative. You have also received input from your peers about how to improve it. Now you are going to revise your draft.

← REVISION GUIDE

Examine your draft to find areas for revision. Keep in mind your purpose and audience as you revise for clarity, development, organization, and style. Use the guide below to help you review.

Review	Revise	Example
Clarity		
Label each piece of dialogue so you know who is speaking. Annotate any places where it is unclear who is speaking.	Use the character's name to show who is speaking or add description about the speaker.	Jimmy looked at me more closely. "You're the kid with the camera? The one who's always taking pictures of the basketball games? My mom, she really loved that picture you took of me making the winning shot. Nice!" ~~He~~ Jimmy held out his fist, and I tapped it with mine.

Please note that excerpts and passages in the StudySync® library and this workbook are intended as touchstones to generate interest in an author's work. The excerpts and passages do not substitute for the reading of entire texts, and StudySync® strongly recommends that students seek out and purchase the whole literary or informational work in order to experience it as the author intended. Links to online resellers are available in our digital library. In addition, complete works may be ordered through an authorized reseller by filling out and returning to StudySync® the order form enclosed in this workbook.

Reading & Writing Companion 123

Review	Revise	Example
Development		
Identify key moments leading up to the climax. Annotate content that doesn't help move the narrative toward the climax or the resolution.	Focus on a single event and think carefully about whether it drives the story forward or keeps it standing still. If it doesn't move the narrative forward, you might consider adding or subtracting details to make it more important to the plot.	~~The~~ Suddenly, the girl standing next to him, Clarice, ~~looked at me thoughtfully. I could tell she was running through her memory bank trying to place me.~~ ~~"Oh yeah! You're Clicks." the girl said.~~ said, "Wait! Jimmy, he *does* go to our school. He's Clicks!" *Clicks?*
Organization		
Explain your story in one or two sentences. Reread and annotate any places that don't match your explanation.	Rewrite the events in the correct sequence. Delete events that are not essential to the story.	A big sigh of relief escaped my lips. It turned out that I wasn't going to get beat up, and I had a nickname that was kind of cool. Who knew? ~~And I wasn't going to get beat up!~~ All this time, people had been thinking of me not as that kid with the scar but as the kid with the camera. Maybe I wasn't such an outsider after all.
Style: Word Choice		
Find places where the use of precise or sensory language can help readers visualize the characters, setting, or action.	Select sentences to rewrite using specific nouns and action verbs or sensory language.	It looks like a couple of ~~lines~~ lightening bolts on my left cheek, and it would look cool on a superhero but not so much on a skinny teenager ~~me~~.

Style: Sentence Effectiveness		
Think about a key event that you want to evoke a specific emotion. Long sentences can draw out a moment and make a reader think; short sentences can show urgent actions or danger.	Rewrite a key event or idea, making your sentences longer or shorter to achieve the emotion you want your reader to feel.	It made me ~~wonder. Maybe~~ wonder if maybe the reason nobody bothered to ask me about my scar anymore wasn't because I fit in~~. Maybe it was~~ but because I always had a camera in front of my face.

 WRITE

Use the guide above, as well as your peer reviews, to help you evaluate your narrative to determine areas that should be revised.

Please note that excerpts and passages in the StudySync® library and this workbook are intended as touchstones to generate interest in an author's work. The excerpts and passages do not substitute for the reading of entire texts, and StudySync® strongly recommends that students seek out and purchase the whole literary or informational work in order to experience it as the author intended. Links to online resellers are available in our digital library. In addition, complete works may be ordered through an authorized reseller by filling out and returning to StudySync® the order form enclosed in this workbook.

Grammar: Prepositions and Prepositional Phrases

Prepositions

A preposition connects a noun or a pronoun to other words in a sentence. A preposition can be a single word. Prepositions of two or three words are called **compound prepositions**. The same word may be used as a preposition in one sentence and as a different part of speech in another sentence.

Common Prepositions					
above	at	by	in	outside	toward
across	before	down	inside	over	under
after	below	during	like	since	until
against	beside	except	of	through	up
along	between	for	on	throughout	with
around	but (except)	from	out	to	within

Compound Prepositions					
according to	apart from	because of	in addition to	instead of	on top of
ahead of	as to	by means of	in spite of	next to	owing to

Example	Explanation
Lennie choked **with pride**. *Of Mice and Men*	The preposition **with** connects the noun *pride* to the word *choked*.

Prepositional Phrases

A prepositional phrase is a group of words that always begins with a preposition. It always ends with a noun or a pronoun. The ending word is called the **object of the preposition**.

Example	Explanation
Outside, even **through the shut window-pane**, the world looked cold. *1984*	The preposition **through** begins the prepositional phrase that ends with the noun **window-pane. Window-pane** is the object of the preposition. The entire prepositional phrase is **through the shut window-pane**.

⟳ YOUR TURN

1. Which preposition should be added to best connect the italicized words?

> Ten chairs were *lined up* _____ *the east wall.*

○ A. pending

○ B. underneath

○ C. along

○ D. This sentence does not need a preposition.

2. Which preposition should be added to best connect the italicized words?

> Todd *looked at* the chairs _____ *a confused expression* on his face.

○ A. unhappily

○ B. with

○ C. between

○ D. This sentence does not need a preposition.

3. Which preposition should be added to connect the italicized words?

> He could not tell the *new chairs* _____ *the old ones.*

○ A. by means of

○ B. apart from

○ C. according to

○ D. This sentence does not need a preposition.

4. Which preposition should be added to connect the italicized words?

> *The old chair squeaked* _____ *a mouse* when he sat down.

○ A. of

○ B. as

○ C. like

○ D. This sentence does not need a preposition.

Please note that excerpts and passages in the StudySync® library and this workbook are intended as touchstones to generate interest in an author's work. The excerpts and passages do not substitute for the reading of entire texts, and StudySync® strongly recommends that students seek out and purchase the whole literary or informational work in order to experience it as the author intended. Links to online resellers are available in our digital library. In addition, complete works may be ordered through an authorized reseller by filling out and returning to StudySync® the order form enclosed in this workbook.

Reading & Writing Companion 127

Grammar: Independent and Dependent Clauses

A clause is a group of words that has both a subject (noun) and a predicate (verb). A clause can function as a sentence by itself or as part of a sentence.

Independent or Main Clause

An independent clause is also called a main clause. An independent or main clause has a subject and a predicate and expresses a complete thought. It can stand alone as a sentence.

Incorrect	Correct
community service	Community service is required.
unless I'm on vacation	I don't sleep late unless I'm on vacation.

Dependent or Subordinate Clause

A dependent clause is also called a subordinate clause. A dependent or subordinate clause has a subject and a predicate, but it does not express a complete thought. It cannot stand alone as a sentence.

Dependent or subordinate clauses usually begin with a subordinating conjunction, such as *when, since, because, after,* or *while*. They may also begin with a relative pronoun, such as *who, whose, whom, which, that,* or *what* or a relative adverb (such as *when, where,* or *why*).

Text	Explanation
And **since she cleaned many houses each week**, we had a great assortment. *The Joy Luck Club*	**Since** is a coordinating conjunction. It begins the dependent clause. **Cleaned** is the verb in the dependent clause. It tells what *she* did.
Any sound **that Winston made**, above the level of a very low whisper, would be picked up by it . . . *1984*	**That** is a relative pronoun. It stands in for the noun *sound*. It begins the dependent clause. **Made** is the verb in the dependent clause. It tells what *Winston* did.

YOUR TURN

1. How should this sentence be changed?

   > Chad devotes more time to his studies he quit his job.

   ○ A. Insert **although** before **Chad**.
   ○ B. Insert **since** after **studies**.
   ○ C. Insert **who** after **Chad**.
   ○ D. No change needs to be made to this sentence.

2. How should this sentence be changed?

   > Although she returned the hiking boots that were too small.

   ○ A. Delete the word **although**.
   ○ B. Replace **that** with **which**.
   ○ C. Insert a comma after **boots**.
   ○ D. No change needs to be made to this sentence.

3. How should this sentence be changed?

   > Whenever we visit the zoo, Emma and I look for the giraffes first.

   ○ A. Delete **whenever**.
   ○ B. Insert a period after **zoo**.
   ○ C. Delete **Emma and I look for the giraffes first**.
   ○ D. No change needs to be made to this sentence.

4. How should this sentence be changed?

   > The computer that Jill had bought last year.

   ○ A. Delete **that**.
   ○ B. Insert **broke** after **year**.
   ○ C. Insert **because** before **the**.
   ○ D. No change needs to be made to this sentence.

Grammar:
Basic Spelling Rules I

Rule	Text	Explanation
When adding a suffix that begins with a vowel to a word that ends with a silent e, usually drop the e.	And surely, to a man of spirit, the **degradation** of cowardice must be **immeasurably** more **grievous** than the unfelt death which strikes him in the midst of his strength and patriotism! History of the Peloponnesian War: Pericles' Funeral Oration	The words *degradation*, *immeasurably*, and *grievous* have suffixes that start with vowels, so the final silent e has been dropped from each word.
Usually, when *i* and *e* appear together in one syllable, the *i* comes before the *e*. When *i* and *e* appear after a *c*, the *e* usually comes before the *i*.	Among the photographs Lange forwarded to Washington was one which soon **achieved** the stature of an American **masterpiece**. Endangered Dreams: The Great Depression in California	The words *achieved* and *masterpiece* follow the spelling pattern of most words, *i* before *e*.
When adding a suffix that begins with *a* or *o* to a word that ends with *ce* or *ge*, usually keep the e.	Because the family unit was **advantageous** for human survival, it became a way of life. Romantic Love: Reality or Myth?	In *advantageous*, the silent e stays put before the suffix *-ous* because *advantage* ends with *ge*.
When a word ends in a consonant + *y*, change the *y* to *i* before adding a suffix. When a word ends in a vowel + *y*, usually keep the *y*.	They interfered with the perfect **ugliness** of the place; they were too **beautiful**; they said too much that we could not understand; they did not make sense. Marigolds	In *ugliness* and *beautiful*, a final *y* has been replaced with *i* before adding a suffix.
Double the final consonant before adding a suffix that begins with a vowel to a word that ends in a single consonant preceded by a single vowel.	And now at the dead hour of the night, amid the dreadful silence of that old house, so strange a noise as this excited me to **uncontrollable** terror. "The Tell-Tale Heart"	In the word *uncontrollable*, the base word *control* ends with a consonant and the suffix *-able* begins with a vowel. Therefore, the final consonant in *control* was doubled.

YOUR TURN

1. How should the spelling error in this sentence be corrected?

> The *Odyssey* is set at a time when warriors committed to obeiing powerful chieftains in return for security and bounty.

- ○ A. Change **obeiing** to **obeying**.
- ○ B. Change **chieftains** to **cheiftains**.
- ○ C. Change **security** to **secureity**.
- ○ D. No change needs to be made to this sentence.

2. How should the spelling error in this sentence be corrected?

> From an early age, Marion Anderson immersed herself in her music, and her determineation paid off because she achieved great things.

- ○ A. Change **immersed** to **imersed**.
- ○ B. Change **determineation** to **determination**.
- ○ C. Change **achieved** to **acheived**.
- ○ D. No change needs to be made to this sentence.

3. How should this sentence be changed?

> Anne's scar is hardly noticable now.

- ○ A. Change **noticable** to **noticeable**.
- ○ B. Change **hardly** to **harddly**.
- ○ C. Change **hardly** to **hardlly**.
- ○ D. No change needs to be made to this sentence.

Please note that excerpts and passages in the StudySync® library and this workbook are intended as touchstones to generate interest in an author's work. The excerpts and passages do not substitute for the reading of entire texts, and StudySync® strongly recommends that students seek out and purchase the whole literary or informational work in order to experience it as the author intended. Links to online resellers are available in our digital library. In addition, complete works may be ordered through an authorized reseller by filling out and returning to StudySync® the order form enclosed in this workbook.

Reading & Writing
Companion

131

Narrative Writing Process: Edit and Publish

PLAN	DRAFT	REVISE	EDIT AND PUBLISH

You have revised your real or imagined narrative based on your peer feedback and your own examination.

Now, it is time to edit your narrative. When you revised, you focused on the content of your narrative. You probably paid attention to your story's narrative techniques and descriptive details. When you edit, you focus on the mechanics of your story, paying close attention to things like grammar and punctuation.

Use the checklist below to guide you as you edit:

☐ Have I followed the rules for prepositions and prepositional phrases?

☐ Have I used independent and dependent clauses?

☐ Have I followed the spelling rules, including those for *ie* and *ei* and adding prefixes and suffixes?

☐ Do I have any sentence fragments or run-on sentences?

☐ Have I spelled everything correctly?

Notice some edits Mason has made:

- Corrected end punctuation of sentences.

- Changed prepositions and prepositional phrases.

- Applied basic spelling rules to correct spelling errors.

- Fixed independent and dependent clauses.

The class picnic was coming up. I decided to go but for once to leave my precious camera at ~~home!~~ home. Without the ~~wieght~~ weight of the camera around my neck, I felt exposed. I put on a ball cap, and that made me feel a little more like ~~myself.~~myself, but you could still see my face. ~~Still see my face.~~ At the picnic, I ~~sit~~ sat near kids I knew from the newspaper, and I talked to some of my teachers, and that was fine. Then, I tried to join a game of softball. That's when I got into trouble. Jimmy, a kid from the basketball team, came up to me and said, "Dude, this game is only for kids who go to our school." I looked around ~~nervously?~~ nervously. I said, "I do go to our school." Jimmy shook his head. He said, "I know everybody in our grade, and I don't know you." He seemed to be ~~geting~~ getting angry.

✏ WRITE

Use the questions on the previous page, as well as your peer reviews, to help you evaluate your narrative to determine areas that need editing. Then edit your narrative to correct those errors.

Once you have made all your corrections, you are ready to publish your work. You can distribute your writing to family and friends, hang it on a bulletin board, or post it on your blog. If you publish online, share the link with your family, friends, and classmates.

Please note that excerpts and passages in the StudySync® library and this workbook are intended as touchstones to generate interest in an author's work. The excerpts and passages do not substitute for the reading of entire texts, and StudySync® strongly recommends that students seek out and purchase the whole literary or informational work in order to experience it as the author intended. Links to online resellers are available in our digital library. In addition, complete works may be ordered through an authorized reseller by filling out and returning to StudySync® the order form enclosed in this workbook.

Reading & Writing Companion **133**

The Christmas Truce of 1914

INFORMATIONAL TEXT

Introduction

World War I was a disastrous war, full of unimaginable agony among the troops. However, early in the war, a remarkable truce occurred. What was it that made enemy troops, for a short while, stop fighting and

ⓥ VOCABULARY

trench
long ditch used by soldiers to stay safe and hidden

truce
an agreement between enemies to stop fighting

tacitly
in a way that is understood or agreed without speaking a word

mutiny
refusal to accept orders; a rebellion

banter
to joke or speak in a playful way

☰ READ

NOTES

1   Every war is a terrible event. World War I was one of the most dreadful. It lasted from 1914 to 1918. More than 25 million people were killed or wounded. At first, people believed the war would end quickly. Fighting would be over by Christmas. It was not. Soldiers would not be home for a long time.

2   Part of the war was waged in Europe. Battles were fought in Belgium and France. Conditions were brutal. The soldiers lived in horrible **trenches**. An area called "no man's land" separated them. The enemy trenches in some places were close. Soldiers could hear the enemy talking.

3   November of the first year came. The war had been on for three months. English and German soldiers were already exhausted. They did not want to fight. They did not want to kill anyone. Some soldiers took on a live and let live attitude. They would **tacitly** agree to stop shooting. Occasionally, the men would **banter** back and forth. Some claim that all this led to the Christmas **truce** of 1914.

NOTES

4   The weather in December of 1914 had been bad. Constant rain soaked everything. Mud was everywhere. Life was horrible. Then a hard frost set in on Christmas Eve. Snow dusted the ground. Perhaps it was this sudden change in weather. Perhaps it was the Christmas season. Somehow war stopped in some parts. And soldiers celebrated the holiday instead.

5   German soldiers lit candles. They put small trees along the trench border. Then something magical happened. The Germans began to sing a Christmas carol. The British soldiers sang one of theirs. Then they joined together to sing "O Come, All Ye Faithful." The British sang in English. The Germans sang in Latin. Singing was also heard on both sides in other places, too.

6   Then on Christmas morning something unusual happened. The men slowly came out of their trenches. They were going to greet the enemy. They were cautious. But no one fired any shots. Men shouted Christmas greetings instead. They exchanged gifts. They took photos. A German soldier even cut the hair of a British soldier. The man had once been a barber. In some places, the men played soccer.

7   Some diaries and letters have survived. They tell of many exchanges among the enemy soldiers. Some say about 100,000 people participated. If the men had been left to themselves, the war would have likely ended. A German soldier called out a message that made sense. He said we are Saxons. You are Anglo-Saxons. What is there to fight about?

8   The truce continued in some areas. It lasted nearly a week. Eventually it ended. The British High Command called associating with the enemy treason. Officers were not to allow soldiers to be friendly. The truce was not official. It could not be allowed. It was illegal. High Command feared that the socializing might continue. That could lead to **mutiny**. It could end the war. It was declared that anyone befriending the enemy would be harshly punished. Commanding officers clearly wanted the war to continue. A German Corporal named Adolf Hitler explained, "Such a thing should not happen in wartime. Have you no German sense of honor?"

9   The men on both sides shared brutal experiences. They could understand each other's pain. They might even have been friends under different circumstances. The Christmas truce was beautiful. It was a moment of happiness.

10   The war continued. Fighting became more savage. Sadly, the truce was never repeated.

First Read

Read the text. After you read, complete the Think Questions below.

1. What two countries are the soldiers from in the text?

   The soldiers are from _____ and _____.

2. Describe the time and place in the text.

   The year is _____. The time of year is _____.

   The place is _____.

3. What historical clues tell us about the truce of 1914?

   We learn about the truce from _____

   _____

   _____

4. Use context to confirm the meaning of the word *tacitly* as it is used in "The Christmas Truce of 1914." Write your definition of *tacitly* here.

   Tacitly means _____.

   A context clue is _____.

5. What is another way to say that two countries signed a *truce*?

   The two countries _____

   _____

Please note that excerpts and passages in the StudySync® library and this workbook are intended as touchstones to generate interest in an author's work. The excerpts and passages do not substitute for the reading of entire texts, and StudySync® strongly recommends that students seek out and purchase the whole literary or informational work in order to experience it as the author intended. Links to online resellers are available in our digital library. In addition, complete works may be ordered through an authorized reseller by filling out and returning to StudySync® the order form enclosed in this workbook.

Reading & Writing Companion 137

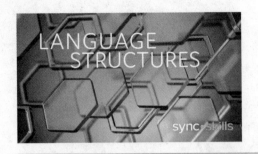

Skill:
Language Structures

★ DEFINE

In every language, there are rules that tell how to **structure** sentences. These rules define the correct order of words. In the English language, for example, a **basic** structure for sentences is subject, verb, and object. Some sentences have more **complicated** structures.

You will encounter both basic and complicated **language structures** in the classroom materials you read. Being familiar with language structures will help you better understand the text.

••• CHECKLIST FOR LANGUAGE STRUCTURES

To improve your comprehension of language structures, do the following:

✓ Monitor your understanding.

- Ask yourself: Why do I not understand this sentence? Is it because I do not understand some of the words? Or is it because I do not understand the way the words are ordered in the sentence?

✓ Break down the sentence into its parts.

- In English, many sentences share this basic pattern: subject + verb + object.

  > The **subject** names who or what is doing the action.

  > The **verb** names the action or state of being.

  > The **object** answers questions such as Who?, What?, Where?, and When?

- Ask yourself: What is the action? Who or what is doing the action? What details do the other words provide?

✓ Confirm your understanding with a peer or teacher.

YOUR TURN

Read the following excerpt from the text. Then complete the multiple-choice questions below.

---

from **"The Christmas Truce of 1914"**

The men on both sides shared brutal experiences. They could understand each other's pain.

---

1. What is the subject of sentence 1?

   ○ A. men
   ○ B. both
   ○ C. sides
   ○ D. experiences

2. Which word names the action in sentence 1?

   ○ A. on
   ○ B. sides
   ○ C. shared
   ○ D. brutal

3. Which word is the object in sentence 2?

   ○ A. could
   ○ B. each
   ○ C. other's
   ○ D. pain

4. Which is the simplest subject-verb-object construction of sentence 2?

   ○ A. They could each other.
   ○ B. They could pain.
   ○ C. Understand other's pain.
   ○ D. They could understand pain.

Please note that excerpts and passages in the StudySync® library and this workbook are intended as touchstones to generate interest in an author's work. The excerpts and passages do not substitute for the reading of entire texts, and StudySync® strongly recommends that students seek out and purchase the whole literary or informational work in order to experience it as the author intended. Links to online resellers are available in our digital library. In addition, complete works may be ordered through an authorized reseller by filling out and returning to StudySync® the order form enclosed in this workbook.

Reading & Writing Companion   **139**

Skill:
Conveying Ideas

 DEFINE

Conveying ideas means communicating a **message** to another person. When speaking, you might not know what word to use to convey your ideas. When you do not know the exact English word, you can try different strategies. For example, you can ask for help from classmates or your teacher. You may use gestures and physical movements to act out the word. You can also try using **synonyms** or **defining** and describing the meaning you are trying to express.

••• CHECKLIST FOR CONVEYING IDEAS

To convey ideas for words you do not know when speaking, use the following learning strategies:

- ✓ Request help.

- ✓ Use gestures or physical movements.

- ✓ Use a synonym for the word.

- ✓ Describe what the word means using other words.

- ✓ Give an example of the word you want to use.

↻ YOUR TURN

Match each example with its correct strategy for conveying the meaning of the word *exhausted*.

A	The person explains that the word means feeling tired right down to your bones.
B	The person mimes struggling to stay upright and awake.
C	The person uses the similar word *fatigued*.
D	The person says it is like when you stay up all night studying and try to stay awake in school the next day.

Strategies	Examples
Use gestures or physical movements.	
Use a synonym for the word.	
Describe what the word means using other words.	
Give examples of the word you want to use.	

Close Read

✏ WRITE

INFORMATIVE: "The Christmas Truce of 1914" is about a time during World War I when soldiers on different sides stopped fighting for the Christmas holiday. Write a paragraph in which you explain why the war was "dreadful" and why the "Christmas Truce" was so special. Use details and events from the text to support your explanation. Pay attention to and edit for spelling patterns and rules.

Use the Checklist below to guide you as you write.

☐ What made the war "dreadful"?

☐ What happened as Christmas arrived?

☐ How was the truce special?

Use the sentence frames to organize and write your informative text.

Every war is dreadful, but _____.

The soldiers lived _____.

Their enemies were _____. The weather was _____.

When Christmas came, some soldiers _____.

They started to _____.

The contrast between the truce and the war was _____.

When Everything Changed

Introduction

I n this poem, a new student comes to school. She is different from her classmates, and sits alone. How will her arrival change two lives?

V VOCABULARY

melody
song or tune

ridicule
make fun of something in a cruel or harsh way

esteemed
highly valued and respected

shelter
building that protects people or animals; home

prom
formal dance given by a high school or college class

☰ READ

1 My mother told me,
2 "Things happen for a reason."
3 She was right.

4 "Class," Ms. Derry said,
5 "meet Bianca Caprelli, a new student.
6 Her family moved here from Italy."

7 After her announcement,
8 We all stared at this outsider.
9 Her clothes,
10 Not our usual uniform of jeans, sassy shirt, sneakers.
11 Her words sang,
12 Almost like a familiar but forgotten **melody**.

13   She didn't belong in our closed world full of giggles,

14   Mockery,

15   Football games,

16   **Proms**.

17   Our tight world belonged to us.

18   We were important,

19   **Esteemed**, and

20   Revered.

21   At lunch, she sat alone,

22   Looking like a frightened deer.

23   The others laughed.

24   They **ridiculed** her clothes.

25   They imitated her accent.

26   They sneered.

27   Their sneering snaked across the room

28   And shattered her.

29   And I . . . I felt sorry for her.

30   On pizza day,

31   I sat down next to her,

32   Breaking the rules of the Others.

33   And they glared at me.

34   "Hi," I said, feeling their sword stares,

35   "I'm Anna. Can I sit with you?"

36   She smiled shyly.

37   She missed Italy and riding her bike in the city.

38   I asked if she wanted a tour of the town after school.

39   She nodded as a smile lit her face.

40   The Others left together,

41   ignoring us.

42   And I knew what they were thinking,

43   And I did not care.

44   That day in the lunchroom was long ago.

45   This afternoon my best friend and I will take our children

46   To volunteer at the animal **shelter**.

47   "Because," Bianca says, "they must learn that all of us need a friend."

48   A lesson I hope they will learn.

Please note that excerpts and passages in the StudySync® library and this workbook are intended as touchstones to generate interest in an author's work. The excerpts and passages do not substitute for the reading of entire texts, and StudySync® strongly recommends that students seek out and purchase the whole literary or informational work in order to experience it as the author intended. Links to online resellers are available in our digital library. In addition, complete works may be ordered through an authorized reseller by filling out and returning to StudySync® the order form enclosed in this workbook.

Reading & Writing
Companion

145

First Read

Read the text. After you read, complete the Think Questions below.

☁ THINK QUESTIONS

1. Who is the new student? What country does she come from?

   The new student is _____.

   She comes from _____.

2. Write a sentence describing the main setting of the poem.

   The poem mostly takes place in _____

   _____.

3. By the end of the poem, what happens to the speaker and the new student? Write two or three sentences to explain their relationship.

   They become _____

   _____

   _____.

4. Use context to confirm the meaning of the word *ridiculed* as it is used in "When Everything Changed." Write your definition of *ridiculed* here.

   Ridiculed means_____.

   A context clue is _____.

5. What is another way to say that a person is *esteemed*?

   A person _____

   _____.

Skill: Analyzing Expressions

★ DEFINE

When you read, you may find English expressions that you do not know. An **expression** is a group of words that communicates an idea. Three types of expressions are idioms, sayings, and figurative language. They can be difficult to understand because the meanings of the words are different from their **literal**, or usual, meanings.

An **idiom** is an expression that is commonly known among a group of people. For example, "It's raining cats and dogs" means it is raining heavily. **Sayings** are short expressions that contain advice or wisdom. For instance, "Don't count your chickens before they hatch" means do not plan on something good happening before it happens. **Figurative** language is when you describe something by comparing it with something else, either directly (using the words *like* or *as*) or indirectly. For example, "I'm as hungry as a horse" means I'm very hungry. None of the expressions are about actual animals.

••• CHECKLIST FOR ANALYZING EXPRESSIONS

To determine the meaning of an expression, remember the following:

✓ If you find a confusing group of words, it may be an expression. The meaning of words in expressions may not be their literal meaning.

- Ask yourself: Is this confusing because the words are new? Or because the words do not make sense together?

✓ Determining the overall meaning may require that you use one or more of the following:

- context clues

- a dictionary or other resource

- teacher or peer support

✓ Highlight important information before and after the expression to look for clues.

YOUR TURN

Read the following excerpt from the text. Then complete the multiple-choice questions below.

---

from **"When Everything Changed"**

The others laughed.
They ridiculed her clothes.
They imitated her accent.
They sneered.
Their sneering snaked across the room
And shattered her.
And I . . . I felt sorry for her.

On pizza day,
I sat down next to her,
Breaking the rules of the Others.
And they glared at me.

"Hi," I said, feeling their sword stares,
"I'm Anna. Can I sit with you?"

---

1. Which line contains figurative language?

   ○ A. They ridiculed her clothes.

   ○ B. They imitated her accent.

   ○ C. They sneered.

   ○ D. Their sneering snaked across the room.

2. What does the poet mean by "shattered her"?

   ○ A. The sneering broke the girl in two.

   ○ B. The sneering made the girl feel terrible.

   ○ C. The sneering was loud enough to break glass.

   ○ D. The sneering broke into pieces over her.

3. Why are the students giving the speaker "sword stares"?

　　○ A. They are angry that she is sitting with the new girl.

　　○ B. They want to hurt her physically by staring at her.

　　○ C. They hope that she will harm the new girl.

　　○ D. They feel that she may be in danger.

4. Which is the best literal meaning of "sword stares"?

　　○ A. pointing fingers

　　○ B. defiant faces

　　○ C. sad looks

　　○ D. angry looks

Please note that excerpts and passages in the StudySync® library and this workbook are intended as touchstones to generate interest in an author's work. The excerpts and passages do not substitute for the reading of entire texts, and StudySync® strongly recommends that students seek out and purchase the whole literary or informational work in order to experience it as the author intended. Links to online resellers are available in our digital library. In addition, complete works may be ordered through an authorized reseller by filling out and returning to StudySync® the order form enclosed in this workbook.

Reading & Writing Companion　　149

Skill: Retelling and Summarizing

★ DEFINE

You can retell and summarize a text after reading to show your understanding. **Retelling** is telling a story again in your own words. **Summarizing** is giving a short explanation of the most important ideas in a text.

Keep your retelling or summary **concise**. Only include important information and key words from the text. By summarizing and retelling a text, you can improve your comprehension of the text's ideas.

••• CHECKLIST FOR RETELLING AND SUMMARIZING

In order to retell or summarize a text, note the following:

✓ Identify the main events of the text.

- Ask yourself: What happens in this text? What are the main events that happen at the beginning, the middle, and the end of the text?

✓ Identify the main ideas in a text.

- Ask yourself: What are the most important ideas in the text?

✓ Determine the answers to the six WH questions.

- Ask yourself: After reading this text, can I answer Who?, What?, Where?, When?, Why?, and How? questions.

YOUR TURN

Read the following excerpt from the text. Then complete the multiple-choice questions below.

---

from **"When Everything Changed"**

On pizza day,
I sat down next to her,
Breaking the rules of the Others.
And they glared at me.

"Hi," I said, feeling their sword stares,
"I'm Anna. Can I sit with you?"
She smiled shyly.
She missed Italy and riding her bike in the city.
I asked if she wanted a tour of the town after school.
She nodded as a smile lit her face.

The Others left together,
ignoring us.
And I knew what they were thinking,
And I did not care.

---

1. Which character would not be included in a summary of these stanzas?

   ○ A. Anna
   ○ B. the new girl
   ○ C. the teacher
   ○ D. the Others

2. Where does the action in these stanzas take place?

   ○ A. in Italy
   ○ B. in a cafeteria
   ○ C. on a bike trip
   ○ D. on a tour of the town

3. Which of these statements reveals the most important idea in this excerpt?

   ○ A. The speaker decides to make friends with the new girl.

   ○ B. The new girl misses her home and wishes she were there.

   ○ C. The speaker's friends do not seem to like the speaker.

   ○ D. The new girl and the speaker both enjoy eating pizza.

4. Which is the best summary of the excerpt?

   ○ A. Anna decides to break the rules. She sits with the new girl. Anna's friends get up and leave the cafeteria in disgust.

   ○ B. Bianca tells Anna about her home in Italy. Anna wants to share her experiences in the town they live in now.

   ○ C. Anna and Bianca eat pizza together in the cafeteria. The other students sneer at them.

   ○ D. The speaker ignores her friends' disgust. She sits with the new girl in the cafeteria. They talk about Italy. They make plans for later.

Close Read

✏ WRITE

NARRATIVE: In the poem "When Everything Changed," Anna shows support for Bianca, a newcomer at her school. Retell the story from Bianca's point of view. How did she feel before meeting Anna? How did Anna make her feel? Use the characters, settings, and sequence of events from the original text. Pay attention to and edit for pronouns and antecedents.

Use the Checklist below to guide you as you write.

☐ How do you (Bianca) feel at the new school?

☐ How does this change when you meet Anna?

Use the sentence frames to organize and write your narrative.

When I first arrived in Ms. Derry's class, I felt _____.

Later, the other kids _____.

Alone in the cafeteria, I felt very _____.

When Anna sat with me, _____.

Today, we are _____.

PHOTO/IMAGE CREDITS:

Cover, ©iStock.com/monkeybusinessimages
Unit Covers, ©iStock.com/eyewave, ©iStock.com/subjug,
©iStock.com/lvantsov, iStock.com/borchee, ©iStock.com/
seb_ra
p. iii, iStock.com/DNY59
p. iv, ©iStock.com/texasmile
p. v, ©iStock.com/texasmile
p. v, iStock.com/deimagine
p. vi, ©iStock.com/texasmile
p. vi, iStock.com/Havana1234
p. vi, iStock.com/bruev
p. vi, iStock.com/Studio-Annika
p. vi, iStock.com/Steve Debenport
p. vi, iStock.com/inhauscreative
p. vii, iStock.com/hanibaram, iStock.com/seb_ra, iStock.
com/Martin Barraud
p. vii, iStock.com/oonal
p. ix, ©iStock.com/monkeybusinessimages
p. x, Jabeen Akhtar - Used by permission of Jabeen
Akhtar
p. x, Brene Brown - NBCUniversal/NBC NewsWire/
Contributor/Getty Images
p. x, Eugenia Collier - Afro Newspaper/Gado/Contributor/
Archive Photos/Getty
p. x, Edwidge Danticat - Patrick McMullan/Contributor/
Patrick McMullan Collection/Getty
p. x, Martin Luther King Jr. - Bettmann/Contributor/
Bettmann/Getty Images
p. xi, Guy De Maupassant - Culture Club/Contributor/
Hulton Archive/Getty
p. xi, Frank McCourt - Anthony Barboza/Contributor/
Archive Photos/Getty
p. xi, Sara Abou Rached - courtesy of Sara Abou Rashed
p. xi, Karen Russell - Pieter M. van Hattem/Contributor/
Contour/Getty
p. 0, ©iStock.com/texasmile
p. 1, Universal History Archive/Universal Images Group/
Getty Images
p. 10, ©iStock.com/Delpixart/
p. 11, ©iStock.com/Delpixart/
p. 12, ©iStock.com/texasmile
p. 13, ©istock.com/urbancow
p. 14, ©istock.com/urbancow
p. 15, ©iStock.com/deimagine
p. 16, ©iStock.com/deimagine
p. 17, ©iStock.com/texasmile
p. 18, ©iStock.com/ramzihachicho
p. 19, Public domain
p. 28, ©iStock.com/ramzihachicho
p. 29, ©iStock.com/Dominique_Lavoie
p. 30, ©iStock.com/Dominique_Lavoie
p. 31, ©iStock.com/ramzihachicho
p. 32, iStock.com/
p. 35, ©iStock.com/chinaface
p. 39, ©istock.com/stargateone
p. 54, ©istock.com/stargateone

p. 55, ©iStock.com/Martin Barraud
p. 56, ©iStock.com/Martin Barraud
p. 57, ©iStock.com/ooyoo
p. 58, ©iStock.com/ooyoo
p. 59, ©istock.com/stargateone
p. 60, ©istock.com/sharply_done
p. 63, ©iStock.com/ollo
p. 68, ©iStock.com/ollo
p. 69, ©iStock.com/
p. 70, ©iStock.com/
p. 71, ©iStock.com/ollo
p. 72, ©iStock.com/FSTOPLIGHT
p. 73, Used by permission of Jabeen Akhtar.
p. 75, Used by permission of Jabeen Akhtar.
p. 83, ©iStock.com/
p. 86, ©iStock.com/AndreyKrav
p. 91, ©iStock.com/AndreyKrav
p. 92, ©iStock.com/DNY59
p. 93, ©iStock.com/DNY59
p. 94, ©iStock/pixhook
p. 95, ©iStock/pixhook
p. 96, ©iStock.com/AndreyKrav
p. 97, ©iStock.com/pernsanitfoto
p. 101, ©iStock.com/Martin Barraud
p. 102, ©iStock.com/Martin Barraud
p. 107, ©iStock.com/oonal
p. 109, ©iStock.com/Martin Barraud
p. 113, ©iStock.com/truelight
p. 115, ©iStock.com/Jinnawat
p. 117, ©iStock/Syldavia
p. 119, ©iStock/Jasmina007
p. 121, ©iStock.com/stevedangers
p. 123, ©iStock.com/Martin Barraud
p. 126, iStock/borchee
p. 128, iStock.com/
p. 130, iStock.com/efks
p. 132, ©iStock.com/Martin Barraud
p. 134, ©iStock.com/Havana1234
p. 135, iStock.com/
p. 135, iStock.com/
p. 135, iStock.com/
p. 135, iStock.com/
p. 135, iStock.com/
p. 137, ©iStock.com/Havana1234
p. 138, ©iStock.com/BlackJack3D
p. 140, ©iStock.com/BlackJack3D
p. 142, ©iStock.com/Havana1234
p. 143, ©iStock.com/KatarzynaBialasiewicz
p. 144, iStock.com/
p. 144, iStock.com/
p. 144, iStock.com/
p. 144, iStock.com/
p. 144, iStock.com/
p. 146, ©iStock.com/KatarzynaBialasiewicz
p. 147, ©iStock.com/Ales_Utovko
p. 150, ©iStock.com/eugenesergeev
p. 153, ©iStock.com/KatarzynaBialasiewicz